Identity and Pedagogy in
Higher Education

Also available from Bloomsbury

Equality in the Secondary School: Promoting Good Practice Across the Curriculum, Mike Cole

Globalization and Internationalization in Higher Education: Theoretical, Strategic and Management Perspectives, Felix Maringe and Nick Foskett

Pedagogy and the University: Critical Theory and Practice, Monica McClean

Identity and Pedagogy in Higher Education

International Comparisons

Kalwant Bhopal and Patrick Alan Danaher

B L O O M S B U R Y

LONDON • NEW DELHI • NEW YORK • SYDNEY

Bloomsbury Academic

An imprint of Bloomsbury Publishing Plc

50 Bedford Square   1385 Broadway
London   New York
WC1B 3DP   NY 10018
UK   USA

www.bloomsbury.com

Bloomsbury is a registered trade mark of Bloomsbury Publishing Plc

First published 2013
Paperback edition published 2014

British Library Cataloguing-in-Publication Data
A catalogue record for this book is available from the British Library.

ISBN: HB: 978-1-4411-2555-2
      PB: 978-1-4725-8224-9
      ePUB: 978-1-4411-8434-4
      ePDF: 978-1-4411-5005-9

Library of Congress Cataloging-in-Publication Data
Bhopal, Kalwant.
Identity and pedagogy in higher education : international comparisons /
Kalwant Bhopal and Patrick Alan Danaher.
p. cm.
Includes bibliographical references and index.
ISBN 978-1-4411-2555-2 (hardcover) – ISBN 978-1-4411-5005-9 (epdf) –
ISBN 978-1-4411-8434-4 (ebook)   1. Discrimination in higher education–Great Britain.
2. Discrimination in higher education–Australia.   I. Danaher, Patrick Alan, 1959–   II. Title.
LC212.3.G7B56   2013
379.2'6–dc23
2012042326

Typeset by Newgen Imaging Systems Pvt Ltd, Chennai, India

Contents

List of Abbreviations

BME	Black and Minority Ethnic
BNP	British National Party
CRT	Critical Race Theory
DfE	Department for Education
DfES	Department for Education and Skills
EAL	English as an Additional Language
ECM	Every Child Matters
GCSE	General Certificate of Secondary Education
HECS	Higher Education Contribution Scheme
HEI	Higher Education Institution
HMSO	Her Majesty's Stationery Office
ITE	Initial Teacher Education
ITT	Initial Teacher Training
NEET	Not in Education, Employment or Training
NQT	Newly Qualified Teachers
OECD	Economic Co-operation and Development
PGCE	Postgraduate Certificate in Education
QTS	Qualified Teacher Status
RAE	Research Assessment Exercise
REF	Research Excellence Framework
TDA	Training and Development Agency

Introduction

This chapter introduces the book by providing an overview of the book and a summary of each chapter. It concludes with a view to exploring issues of 'race' and identity by providing a new theoretical perspective on understanding these key concepts from an international perspective, specifically focusing on student experiences in higher education in the UK and Australia.

The focus on Whiteness, as opposed to Blackness, as a subject of inquiry and analysis in its own right has recently become a popular theme within academic understandings of 'race', identity and Otherness. However, such research has primarily focused on the USA; this book examines the social construction and maintenance of Whiteness within higher educational settings in the UK and Australia. By concentrating on higher education, we specifically explore the relationship between students' experiences of 'race' and their multiple identities within an educational context that has often been neglected.

Although it is different in terms of historical and social contexts, Australia, like the UK, has a complex relationship to and understandings of 'race' (Dunn, Forrest, Pe-Pua, Hynes, & Maeder-Han, 2009; Markus, 2001; Moreton-Robinson, 2004; Russell, 2006). There is little research that takes a comparative perspective in interrogating understandings of identity and its meanings in different cultural environments. This book examines such understandings by focusing on pre-service and postgraduate teacher trainee students' understandings of Whiteness and Blackness. Leonardo (2002, p. 31) argues that 'Whiteness is a racial discourse, whereas the category "white people" represents a socially constructed identity'. To understand Whiteness, however, there is also a need to understand concepts of Blackness and Otherness (Reay et al., 2007). Bonnett (1997) has indicated that Whiteness has developed into a taken-for-granted experience structured upon a varying set of supremacist assumptions (sometimes cultural, sometimes biological, sometimes moral, sometimes all three). Non-White identities, by contrast, have been denied the privileges of normativity, and are marked within the West as marginal and inferior (Bonnett, 1997, p. 188).

Hence this book provides an original, comparative understanding of racialized and gendered student experiences in two differing contexts: those of the UK and of Australia. It explores the ways in which identities are understood and conceptualized in two different, yet broadly similar, cultural and political climates. Further, by investigating these identities in the global and local contexts of higher education, this book aims to bridge a much-needed gap in educational and social scientific research. Of particular contextual focus for this book are two key drivers for the expansion of higher education locally and globally. First, the fact that there remains a belief in some quarters that higher education can provide the tools for greater social equity between and among genders, 'races' and social classes needs to be explored more critically (David, 2007; Zajda et al., 2008). And secondly, while the push towards the internationalization of higher education as an industry has brought some financial relief for the global university sector, this has led to a rise in the numbers of overseas students without either adequate support or the necessary reforms to the higher education curriculum (Dunne, 2011; Luxon & Peelo, 2009; Marginson, 2004). In this book, then, we examine the experiences of local and international students within this context and as a result offer suggestions for viable policy shifts in this area.

The key focus of our book is based on the premise that 'race' is a controversial subject in which difficult and contested discourses are the norm. The purpose of this book and the coherence of its arguments are dictated by an examination of controversial issues, by engaging with empirical data and theoretical debates, within educational research around issues of 'race', identity, culture and inclusion (Anderson & Williams, 2000; Arber, 2008; Ladson-Billings & Gillborn, 2004; Leonardo, 2005; Shih & Sanchez, 2009). The book explores the complexities of 'race', gender and identity within the context that education continues to be dominated by primarily White, middle-class values and perspectives (Youdell, 2006). We agree with Tomlinson (2005, p. 182) that efforts to eliminate 'racial and gender inequality' are 'patchy and uneven' and generally there is an issue that racism in the education system has not been dealt with directly or adequately in the UK or in Australia. This is demonstrated by current policy and practice in the respective education systems in the UK (Ball, 2008) and in Australia (Caluya, Probyn, & Vyas, 2011). Accordingly, our book examines education as a vehicle for change in the light of these debates by drawing on understandings of social inclusion and social justice from the viewpoints of teacher training students and to a lesser extent of academic staff members.

Thus the main aims of the book are to:

- Examine specific areas of discrimination and disadvantage such as 'race', identity and gender within education as well as debating the difficulties of such concepts in relation to the experiences of students in higher education.
- Take a comparative perspective by focusing on the experiences of local and international higher education students in the UK and those in Australia. It analyses contesting discourses of identity in these different cultural contexts.
- As the recent protests in Australia by overseas Indian students over the quality of teaching and support in the higher education sector and over concerns about their safety point out (Dunn, Pelleri, & Maeder-Han, 2011; Robertson, 2011), there is a real urgency to engage more directly with the diverse needs of students.

Research in the UK

There is a growing body of research that examines the ability and willingness of trainee or pre-service teachers (the terms used respectively in the UK and Australia) to understand and engage in issues associated with 'race', diversity, inclusion and identity in the classroom (Ambe, 2006; Santoro & Allard, 2005). These studies (mainly drawn from areas such as North America, Europe and Australasia) show a mismatch between the ethnic identity of the teaching population (which is predominantly White and in some cases it has been pointed out female and middle class) and that of the student intake (which is increasingly becoming ethnically mixed). The identity of teachers and its relationship to the educational achievement of some minority ethnic groups has been pointed out. For example, Rhamie's (2007) research highlights how many African-Caribbean pupils have negative experiences at school in which they receive little support and encouragement from teachers and in which they perceive a sense of being treated differently from their White peers. Similarly, the first phase of a larger project found that Year 8 pupils' complex understandings of identity, diversity and Britishness were summed up in the telling phrase, 'Stick to your own kind' (Rhamie, Bhopal, & Bhatti, 2012). Furthermore, recent research (Bhopal, 2010) has shown that many Asian women in British universities feel excluded and marginalized based on the cultural expectations of their (White) lecturers – that they will not continue with higher education but will leave to have an 'arranged marriage'. To counter this, some minority ethnic women draw on their support networks as strategies of success to enable them to achieve high grades and compete with their White counterparts.

There have been some attempts to address concerns about these issues. This has included a focus on teacher training or teacher education courses (respectively the terms used in the UK and Australia) and the development of programmes to encourage trainee teachers to understand issues associated with 'race', diversity and educational inclusion (see Causey, Thomas, & Armento, 2000; Mills, 2008, 2009). Much of the research has focused on identifying misconceptions and preconceptions around 'race' and diversity (see Garcia & Lopez, 2005). Korthagen et al. (2001) argue that it is possible to work with trainee teachers only after they themselves know that their own stereotypes have to be challenged. However, other researchers have shown that the impact of such interventions is not so effective, but can be quite limiting (Hollins & Guzman, 2005; Sleeter, 2001). The reasons for this remain complex, but part of the problem may be that the lecturers and tutors themselves may not be particularly knowledgeable about such issues and so may lack the confidence to support trainee teachers effectively.

Black and minority ethnic students and teacher training courses

The recruitment and retention of Black and Minority Ethnic (BME) students into Initial Teacher Training (ITT) programmes have been raised as a cause for concern, specifically at policy level (Bhopal, Harris, & Rhamie, 2009). Basit et al.'s small-scale research (2006) found that some BME trainees had experienced racism in school placements. Blair (2001) has argued the need to teach trainees about their own agency in addressing the experiences of BME students – particularly around the stereotypes associated with 'Black failure and exclusions'. Yet recent studies have also examined how trainees should think about their own White, middle-class identities when teaching students from BME backgrounds (Allard & Santoro, 2006; Gazeley & Dunne, 2007). The recent survey of new qualified teachers (Training and Development Agency, 2010) found that a minority of respondents felt that they had not been prepared in their teacher training programmes to teach students from BME backgrounds.

Gazeley and Dunne (2008) in their research found that some tutors felt that the achievement of BME students could be understood only in relation to Black history, culture and integration. They argue that it is crucial to examine the attitudes of teachers, particularly in relation to different aspects of professional practice in schools. They state, 'There is clearly a difference between preparing teachers to work in a society that is ethnically, culturally and economically diverse and promoting teacher trainees' understanding of the relationship between educational outcomes and race equality' (p. 10). Their research also found that, even when there were large numbers of BME groups in the populations and areas, many of the trainee teachers indicated that they lacked sufficient experience of diversity to feel confident about their teaching or thinking about this issue in their future teaching practice. Furthermore, many of the tutors indicated that the teaching of diversity was confined to aspects of the course that covered diversity in general terms such as 'race', class and gender being examined together.

Gazeley and Dunne (2008) also found that most of the teacher trainees seemed confident when talking about 'race' and diversity in relation to their own teaching subjects, specifically in terms of how they adapted their teaching in order to take account of the different ethnic and cultural identities of pupils. Some also indicated that they had been given guidance about addressing issues of racism and how to deal with racist incidents. Yet many found talking about issues of racism difficult and uncomfortable. The authors conclude that more opportunities are needed to examine the impact of professional attitudes and assumptions about the behaviour of BME pupils (e.g. specifically around negative stereotypes).

The DfES has argued that the focus on diversity and inclusion must be strengthened: 'Work with the TDA (Training and Development Agency)[1] to strengthen coverage of race equality issues (and their relationship to effective behaviour management) in all relevant strands of ITT' (DfES, 2006a, p. 27). As Gazeley and Dunne (2008) state:

> Importantly teacher trainees highlighted the importance of professional attitudes in their discussion. ITT programmes occupy a particularly important space within this policy agenda as it is within ITT programmes that attitudes and assumptions are explored and that understandings of such key concepts as race equality and inclusive practice are established. (p. 15)

Recruitment and retention

There has been much concern regarding the recruitment and retention of BME students into the teaching profession (Basit & McNamara, 2004). Research has found that discrimination takes place both at the point of recruitment and promotion and when there is the issue of trainees 'fitting in' (Ahmad et al., 2003). Basit and McNamara (2004) report that respondents in their research said that the greatest advantage for being a minority ethnic teacher was to be a role model for students and to be able to challenge stereotypes towards minority ethnic people and teachers. Another advantage was that it enabled them to have greater insight into cultural and religious understandings that would help to enhance colleagues' understanding of these issues. They also felt that they could communicate more with minority ethnic parents and pupils. The research argues that, if we want to increase the numbers of minority ethnic teachers, more support is required if they are to be recruited and retained. In a further paper, Basit et al. (2006) found that many trainees withdrew from teacher training courses owing to personal and family reasons; but some did so because of experiences of racism (see also Basit & Santoro, 2011).

Gordon (2000) has argued that minority ethnic teachers are important as they can contribute to the experiences of minority ethnic children in the classroom in relation to multiculturalism. The numbers of minority ethnic students who decide to take up teaching is much lower than the national percentage of minority ethnic people in the population and the withdrawal rates for these groups are higher than those of others (Basit et al., 2006). Furthermore, racism has been recognized as one of the reasons that they choose not to go into teacher training (Roberts et al., 2002). Roberts et al. (2002) also found that many trainees speak about being treated less favourably than their peers, specifically in relation to culture and language. Cockburn and Haydn (2004) state that the recruitment and retention of minority ethnic teachers are a major challenge because we need people from all sections of society to want to become teachers. By contrast, Pathak (2000) argues that education is the subject least likely to be studied by ethnic minorities; they are more likely to opt for ostensibly more professional subjects such as law and medicine. Carrington and Skelton (2003) assert that the education system will benefit from minority ethnic teachers owing to their understandings of racism and their ability to act as advocates in school settings. Yet Basit et al. (2006) found that some of the trainees in their research withdrew from courses owing to being victims of deliberate racial harassment in their ITT institutions. Some said that their course tutors were perpetrators of deliberate harassment, while others indicated that they were deliberately given placements in poor schools or those that were far away from where they lived (Basit et al., 2007).

Barrington (2000) notes that Newly Qualified Teachers (NQTs) may need reassurance during the early stages of teaching and training so that they are able to deal with issues of diversity. Hopkins et al. (1998) state that teacher development is most effective in schools that encourage pedagogical partnerships that work to prevent professional isolation and to facilitate 'good practice'. But Wilkins (2001) has argued that trainees feel that exposure to other cultural influences in a multicultural society is sufficient to promote their understandings of diversity.

Some teacher trainees report that they have been 'ethnically matched' to particular schools because of their minority ethnic backgrounds and those in all-White schools have shown that they are isolated in these placements (Carrington et al., 2001). Chambers et al. (2002) have found that the breakdown in trainees' relationships with their mentors was also a major factor in their decisions to withdraw.

Diversity and teacher training

Research carried out by Davies and Crozier (2006) examined the extent of training provision in England regarding issues to do with diversity, 'race' and inclusion. This large-scale piece of research was based on three different strands: questionnaires, telephone interviews and vignettes. Questionnaires were sent to all ITT providers in England, follow-up interviews were conducted with a sample of questionnaire respondents and four providers were identified as having 'interesting practice'. Each of them was visited over a period of two to three days. The findings suggest that the majority of trainees had policies relating to equality and diversity but policies for tackling racism in schools were not consistent across the board. Furthermore, 'race' and diversity were addressed in relation to students with English as an Additional Language (EAL), and there was little coverage of these issues when students were in all-White Higher Education Institutions (HEIs). The majority of respondents in this study felt that there was a need for further development in this area. Many of the Initial Teacher Education (ITE) providers employed generic lectures and key readings and the use of visiting speakers to address issues of diversity. Some said that diversity permeated the curriculum, while others said that it needed further development. Many of the programmes did not address racism, underachievement or teacher expectations, although some providers did refer to the Race Relations Amendment Act (RRA, 2000) but did not require the trainees to consider the implications of the RRA for their own practice.

Davies and Crozier (2006) suggest that 'race' and anti-racism need to be addressed overtly on ITE programmes, and discussing issues to do with 'race' cannot be an 'add on' or a tokenistic response or measure. Furthermore, trainees have to think about the relevance of 'race' to their teaching practice and ITE providers must consider the impact of the requirements of the RRA on their training. It was also suggested that there should be effective monitoring of such equalities policies.

The recruitment and retention of BME trainees into courses were also a cause for concern. On the one hand this was seen as an advantage but on the other hand the targets set by institutions were seen as being unrealistic. There were insufficient advice and guidance in this area and there was a crucial need for continuing professional development in 'race' and diversity for all trainees as well as consistency across the programmes. Davies and Crozier (2006) also suggest, 'Providers need to be more proactive in addressing racism and be more mindful of its impact on teaching and achievement regardless of context or make up of student cohort' (p. 6). They also stress the need to broaden the definition of diversity, particularly in relation to social class, refugees, asylum seekers and Gypsy Traveller and Roma pupils.

Research in Ireland (Hagan & McGlynn, 2004) has also shown that, although trainees generally felt that diversity was an important issue, many did not feel comfortable or that they could deal with diversity issues in the classroom. In Ireland, research has shown that teachers need to adopt a more critical multicultural approach to their teaching in order to meet the challenges posed by a diverse and changing society (McGlynn, 2003). Stoer and Cortesao (2000) suggest that monocultural teachers must transform their thinking for a multicultural society in order to teach effectively in heterogeneous schools, but Le Roux (2002) warns that this presents a huge challenge for trainees.

Multiculturalism, social justice and inclusion in schools

Inclusion

Inclusion is a complex term and, when examining issues of inclusion in the curriculum, researchers (Richardson & Wood, 2000) have argued that inclusion is about the atmosphere and ethos of the school itself. It represents and respects the individual and personal identities of its pupils as well as acknowledging that racism exists and is a part of the lives of many pupils who attend schools. Richardson and Wood (2000) explore the concept of institutional racism along four dimensions: exclusion and non-participation; discrimination (direct and indirect); violence and harassment; and prejudice and hostility owing to attitudes and assumptions. They argue that these are some of the issues that schools should be concerned with when discussing aspects of inclusion.

Social justice and diversity

Zeichner (2001) argues that teachers should in their everyday teaching think about how their teaching affects issues of social justice in relation to social class, religion, gender and other differences. However, there is little research that examines how this reflection can actually happen (Brookfield, 1995; Phelan, 1997). Being reflexive means that teachers must think about their own practice in relation to their own beliefs and principles in the classroom (Serafini, 2003). However, research has shown that teachers are unlikely to be reflexive about their practice, even though they know that this is part of 'good practice' (Shannon & Crawford, 1998). Clarke and Drudy (2007) contend that there is great variation among student teachers regarding issues to do with social justice and diversity; many of them were conservative in their own teaching styles and the question that arises from this is whether teachers themselves are best placed to understand the diversity needs of their students. Holden's research (2003) found that, even though student teachers are committed to teaching about social justice issues, they themselves lack the confidence to do so in the classroom, particularly when they think that the issues may be highly controversial. Furthermore, many student teachers enter teaching with little knowledge or experience of diversity issues and of their own cultural histories (Cockrell et al., 1999).

Clarke and Drudy (2006) state that the importance of social justice and diversity issues for student teachers varies and that the majority of student teachers rely on traditional teaching strategies, a situation that has also been found to occur in the USA (Desforges, 1995). Few student teachers conceptualize social justice in relation to understanding polices that would change society towards a situation of equity (Nussbaum, 2003; Sen, 2002). It has been recognized that trainee teachers from minority ethnic backgrounds face greater problems of racism and discrimination than do their White counterparts (Basit et al., 2006; Powney et al., 2003). It has been argued that positive role models – that is, teachers from minority ethnic backgrounds – can help to enhance the experiences of pupils from minority ethnic backgrounds (Cork, 2005).

Research in the USA

Multiculturalism

There has been a great deal of research in the USA that has examined the effects of multiculturalism, inclusion and diversity in the classroom. However, it has been argued that in the USA there is not a single unified approach to multiculturalism and its teaching in the classroom (Sleeter & Grant, 2009). Gibson (1976) has identified five different approaches to multiculturalism: education of the culturally different (which aims to incorporate students from different cultural backgrounds into mainstream society and culture); education about cultural differences (which teaches students about cultural differences); education for cultural pluralism (to preserve ethnic cultures and increase the power of minority groups); bicultural education (which enables students to operate mutually in two different cultures); and teaching students that multiculturalism is the norm.

Other researchers, however, have focused more on what they call 'anti-oppressive education'. For example, Kumashiro (2002) has elaborated four different approaches to 'anti-oppressive education': education for the 'other' (improving education for those who are marginalized); education about the other (so that the curriculum adequately represents minority ethnic groups); critical education (changing institutions of oppression for more equality); and education that changes oppression in schools' and students' views.

Koppelman and Goodhart define multiculturalism as 'a commitment to pluralism; its guiding purpose is to prepare students to be active participants in a diverse multicultural society' (2005, p. 292). According to Gorski (2000), the underlying goal of multiculturalism is to effect social change through transformation of the self, of schools and of society. Multicultural education proposes that the curriculum should be changed to incorporate a diversity of perspectives and approaches, specifically in relation to the experiences of different groups (Grant & Sleeter, 2002; Nieto, 2001; Sleeter, 2005). In this respect the curriculum should reflect the different perspectives of the students. Nieto (2001) states that multicultural education is a process of school reform that 'permeates the curriculum and instructional strategies used in schools, as well as the interactions among teachers, students and parents, and the very way that schools conceptualize the nature of teaching and learning' (p. 307).

According to Sleeter and Grant (2009), a multicultural approach should include: a reworking of the curricula to include the experiences of all students; the development of a multilingual society; a reworking of teaching processes in the classroom so that they support diversity in the production of knowledge; a reworking of tests so that they are based on what the students have been taught in the curriculum; maintaining a strong relationship between the school and the community (home); and including additional school-wide practices within the approach (e.g. staffing should reflect the student population in terms of ethnic make-up). Berlak and Moyenda (2001) maintain, however, that the main focus of critical multiculturalism 'is naming and actively challenging racism and other forms of injustice, not simply recognising and celebrating differences and reducing prejudice' (p. 92).

Sleeter and Grant (2009) emphasize the importance of examining multiculturalism in relation to social justice, which

> ... starts with the premise that equity and justice should be goals for everyone and that solidarity across differences is needed to bring about justice. The notions of equity and justice point to not just a goal of equal opportunity but also to one of equal results for diverse communities. (pp. 197–8)

The influential work of Sonia Nieto (2010) in her recent research has argued that multiculturalism should be based on three objectives: tackling inequality in education and promoting access to provide an equal education for all; raising the achievement of all students and providing them with a high-quality education; and giving students the opportunity to become critical members of society (p. 44). She states that these goals are crucial because:

> If multicultural education does not tackle the far more thorny questions of stratification and inequity, and if viewed in isolation from the reality of students' lives, these goals can turn into superficial strategies that only scratch the surface of educational failure. (p. 45)

Nieto (2010) also asserts that multiculturalism should aim to promote democracy and contribute to a better society. For Nieto, equality, equity and social justice are crucial elements in the teaching of multicultural education. Social justice is based on challenging stereotypes that lead to discrimination based on 'race', gender, class, etc.; it is based on providing students with the resources that they need to reach their full potential in education; it is based on the perspective that all students (regardless of their backgrounds) can contribute something to education such as their languages, backgrounds and experiences; and the final aspect of social justice is the focus on creating a learning environment in which students are able to think critically for social change.

In order for multiculturalism to be effective, Nieto (2010) states that it has to be anti-racist, related to social justice and based on critical pedagogy. There is sometimes an assumption that, because a school is multicultural, it will be anti-racist in its delivery of multiculturalism. But Nieto argues that this is not always the case. Instead schools that are committed to multiculturalism must examine their policies and the attitudes of staff members to explore how these could discriminate against students, Furthermore, parts of the curriculum must confront racism in the curriculum and schools must create an environment that enables students to discuss openly issues to do with inequality. It is also important for teachers to understand the impact of racism on the classroom. Research has found that in classrooms many teachers actually deny the existence of racism and the effects that it has on pupils and schools (Donaldson, 2001). As Cochran-Smith states,

> To teach lessons about race and racism in teacher education is to struggle to unlearn racism itself – to interrogate the assumptions that are deeply embedded in the curriculum, to our own complicity in maintaining existing systems of privilege and oppression, and to grapple with our own failure. (2000, p. 59)

In order for multiculturalism to be effective, Nieto (2010) insists that it must be aimed at *all* students and teachers. 'White students receive only a partial education, which helps to legitimate their cultural blindness. Seeing only themselves, they may believe that they are the norm and thus most important and everyone else is secondary and less important' (p. 74). Furthermore, multiculturalism has to be part of the ethos and attitudes of the whole school community: 'A true multicultural approach is pervasive. It permeates everything; the school climate, physical environment, curriculum and relationships among teachers and students and community' (p. 75).

According to Nieto (2010), multicultural education is important for achieving social justice in society so that students and teachers can contribute to changes in schools. 'Multicultural education invites students and teachers to put their learning into action for social justice' (p. 76). The processes of multiculturalism are complex and ongoing. She states, '. . . future teachers need to develop an awareness of the influence of culture and language on learning, the persistence of racism and discrimination in schools and society, and instructional and curricular strategies that encourage learning among a wide variety of students' (p. 78). She recognizes that this process is 'complex, problematic, controversial, and time consuming, but it is one in which teachers and schools must engage to make their schools truly multicultural' (p. 78).

There is a variety of different approaches to and perspectives on multicultural education (Banks & Banks, 2004). There have been many developments of multicultural education. The most influential has been the need to engage in a critical pedagogy and to examine the discourse of Whiteness and how White identities become normalized in schools and in society (Ramsey & Williams, 2003).

Social justice

Social justice as a concept has been analysed from different perspectives (Gewirtz, 1998; Ladson-Billings, 1995; Sturman, 1997). Social justice and its meanings have also taken centre stage in the literature on social justice and teacher training (McDonald, 2007), yet it has been argued that most teacher training programmes which use the term do not adequately define it (McDonald & Zeichner, 2009). There are also other approaches that have used the teaching of social justice through Critical Race Theory (CRT) and critical multiculturalism (Gillborn, 2009; Ladson-Billings, 2005; Wiedman, 2002). There are three types of theories that examine the concept of social justice; distributive theories that examine the distribution of goods and services (Rawls, 2001); recognition theories that examine social relations among individuals and groups (Young, 1990); and those that examine both distributive and relational perspectives (Fraser, 1997).

One of the approaches that has been identified by teacher educators to provide a social justice teaching agenda is by providing teachers with a culturally aware and responsive teaching curriculum (Irvine, 2003; Ladson-Billings, 1995). Others have argued that teaching for social justice should include a strong commitment to teachers acting as agents of social change in their teaching both inside and outside schools (Darling-Hammond & Bransford, 2005). In relation to 'race', Zeichner (2009) argues that there are two strands that have focused on social justice: through increasing recruitment of BME students to teacher training; and through developing strategies to promote social justice through teaching styles and the curriculum.

It has been argued that a more diverse teaching population is needed to meet the needs of a diverse intake of students (Villegas & Davis, 2008), and that a diverse staff body is needed to create learning conditions conducive to providing social justice agendas (Sleeter, 2007). However, despite efforts to increase the diversity of teacher trainers in the USA, the intake remains predominantly White, monolingual and English (Zumwalt & Craig, 2005). Furthermore, universities and colleges face difficulties in retaining non-White students (Villegas & Davis, 2008), and the focus on diversity and social justice education in teacher training programmes has been seen as being aimed at preparing White students to teach students of colour (Sleeter, 2001).

Research has found that when social justice is taught within programmes (rather than restricted to specific courses) it is more effective (Moule, 2005). Some examples of how the teaching of social justice has been effective include enabling student teachers to speak about racism and White privilege by examining their own personal biographies and experience (something that many may not have previously thought about) (McIntyre, 2002). There is also evidence to show that teacher educators have to be cautious *where* they place student teachers, as in some cases where student teachers are placed helps to build their understandings of diversity and inclusion through cultural sensitivity, yet in other cases such placements can reinforce the already held and sometimes stereotypes of groups that student teachers had previously held (Haberman & Post, 2008).

Diversity

Gurin et al. (2002) argue that different types of diversity have to be addressed in order for it to be effective in teaching: structural diversity, informal interactional diversity and classroom diversity. Moreover, 'We contend that students educated in diverse institutions will be more motivated and better able to participate in an increasingly heterogeneous and complex society' (p. 339). Similarly, Orfield (2001) has found that there are a variety of individual, institutions and societal benefits that linked to diversity.

There has been a huge change in the ethnic make-up of communities across the world (Santoro, 2009). In Australia, the teaching population has been identified as predominantly White and middle class (Allard & Santoro, 2006). This trait has also been identified in the USA (Chubbuck, 2010; Milner, 2010). It has been argued that, while the student population is becoming more diverse, the teacher trainers are not (Ambe, 2006). Accordingly there is a great need for trainers to understand the diversity of student population in an increasingly multicultural society (Gay, 2010).

Research has shown that teachers are not well prepared to teach diverse students whose cultural values are different from their own (Santoro, 2009), and that many White teachers hold negative stereotypical views about minority ethnic children and have little knowledge of cultural diversity (Sleeter, 2008). Such trainees then attribute those children's academic failure to home and cultural backgrounds, rather than questioning their own pedagogies (Chubbuck, 2010; Sleeter, 2008). Many programmes that try to deal with diversity are simply 'add ons' that do not deal directly with issues of diversity and inclusion (McDonald, 2005). As society is becoming more and more diverse, the teacher population must reflect this diversity if it is to take seriously the notion of social justice and multiculturalism. The qualities that teachers should have include 'a sense of mission, solidarity with, and empathy for their students, the courage to challenge mainstream knowledge, improvisation and a passion for social justice' (Nieto, 2006, p. 463).

Research has found that few courses on teacher training in the USA facilitate teachers' understandings of race, diversity and culture (Ladson-Billings, 1990). By contrast, through engagement in diversity focused teacher training courses, pre-service teachers can gain greater critical insight into the effects of diversity upon teaching and learning (Ladson-Billings, 1995).

Research in Australia

Australia's experiences of and engagements with the issues central to the aims of this book are broadly similar to those already discussed in the UK and the USA, yet they are also distinctive in their own right. Like the UK and the USA, Australia has undergone rapid social change and has witnessed significant racial and ethnic tensions. At the same time, Australia's historical development and contemporary governance constitute a particular set of contexts for understanding and potentially transforming the roles, rights and responsibilities of minority ethnic communities as well as mainstream society. These contexts also create a specific framework for the design and enactment of the curricula and pedagogies of current pre-service teacher training that will have a significant impact on the future life chances and opportunities of minority ethnic learners. As with the two preceding sections of the chapter, these introductory remarks about that framework have been clustered around the three organizing themes of multiculturalism, social justice and diversity.

Multiculturalism

Like the UK and the USA, Australia is from many perspectives undoubtedly a multicultural nation. These perspectives include changing demographics, cultural practices and government policies. Yet understandings of what Australian multiculturalism means vary widely, ranging from sociocultural diversity (Acker, 2008) to a crucial interdependence with social capital (Pardy & Lee, 2011) to liberal individualism and nationalism (Levey, 2008) to a strategic disguise of the real power of the dominant Anglo-Australian culture (Rodrigues, 2003). Certainly a recurring discourse about Australian multiculturalism is that it is – at least potentially and theoretically – a vehicle for national inclusion and a celebration of diversity and cultural pluralism (Boese & Phillips, 2011; Moran,

2011; Smolicz & Secombe, 2009). At the same time, multiculturalism in Australia remains a highly contested and in some ways a deeply divided (and in some quarters divisive) proposition (Jakubowicz, 2011; Whitford, 2011).

Multiculturalism and racism have competed for control as dominant discourses throughout Australia's colonial and postcolonial histories. There were well-documented atrocities committed by the invading/settling British alongside genuine efforts on both sides to understand the inhabitants of 'the other side of the frontier' (Reynolds, 2006). Subsequent landmarks in the multiple histories of Australian race relations have included anti-Chinese riots in the gold rushes of the 1850s and 1860s, the Immigration Restriction Act of 1901 and the associated elements of the White Australia Policy, the settlement of large numbers of Greek and Italian immigrants in the aftermath of World War II, overwhelming public support for the 1967 referendum approving amendments to the Australian constitution with regard to Australian Aboriginal people, the 1992 Australian High Court decision overturning the British colonialist proposition that Australia had been *terra nullius* (land belonging to no-one) and the apology by former Australian prime minister Kevin Rudd in Federal Parliament on 13 February 2008 to Indigenous Australians for the 'stolen generations' (see also Young & Zubrzycki, 2011). As well as being significant elements of Australia's national narratives, each of these is part of the subject matter with which Australian pre-service teachers need to engage as part of their preparations for their future teaching careers.

In Australia, early childhood, primary (elementary), secondary and technical and further education are provided by the respective state and territory governments, and university education by the national government, although the Commonwealth Government has exercised increasing influence over key aspects of their delivery. For example, successive federal governments, both Australian Labor Party and Coalition (Liberal and National Parties), have pushed for the establishment of what is currently known as the 'Australian Curriculum' (www.australiancurriculum.edu.au/). Currently this curriculum consists of four 'learning areas' (English, mathematics, science and history), seven 'general capabilities' (literacy, numeracy, information and communication technology capability, critical and creative thinking, personal and social capability, ethical behaviour and intercultural understanding) and three 'cross-curriculum priorities' (Aboriginal and Torres Strait Islander histories and cultures, Asia and Australia's engagement with Asia and sustainability). Subsequent chapters explore further the Australian Curriculum's potential implications for pre-service teacher training to promote pedagogies that are attentive to 'race', gender and other dimensions of identities, including multiculturalism.

Social justice

Like multiculturalism, social justice is subject to the play of competing claims and divergent discourses in Australia that have significant implications for pre-service teacher training. From one perspective, schooling and higher education alike are seen as complicit with strategies that marginalize members of minority ethnic communities and other disadvantaged learners (Gale & Densmore, 2000). For example, 'the present market-driven goals of higher education' (Joseph, 2012, p. 239) in Australia have been identified as an obstacle to internationalizing the curriculum in ways that respect student diversity and promote social justice. This is similar to a view of the Australian criminal justice system as being inimical to the interests of women who have been physically and sexually abused, with a preference instead for restorative (social) justice strategies (van Wormer, 2009).

From another perspective, by contrast, schooling and higher education can be the sites of developing and mobilizing pedagogical practices that disrupt this hegemony and create alternative and more empowering experiences and opportunities for minority learners. Examples of these practices include 'funds of knowledge, vernacular or local literacies; place-based education; the "productive pedagogies" and the "unofficial curriculum" of popular culture and out-of-school learning settings' (Hattam, Brennan, Zipin, & Comber, 2009, p. 303). Furthermore, using transformative texts in children's literature has been demonstrated as being effective in teaching for social justice in Australian preschools (Hawkins, 2010). Moreover, problem-based learning allied with dialogic learning is employed in several Indigenous Australian studies classrooms as a way of promoting dialogue between Indigenous and non-Indigenous Australian students (Mackinlay & Barney, 2011). More broadly, 'a relational understanding of social justice – "recognitive justice"' is posited as being crucial 'in the context of the planned shift from mass to universal participation' (Gale & Tranter, 2011, p. 29) in Australian higher education.

Given these divergences and sometimes contradictions among approaches to and conceptions of social justice in Australian higher education, it is hardly surprising that there is an equivalent diversity of understandings of and teachings about social justice in Australian pre-service teacher training. On the one hand, specific elements of selected teacher training programmes have been proposed as exhibiting particular social justice principles and also as being successful in assisting prospective teachers to teach about and for social justice in their future careers (Malone et al., 2003; Reynolds & Brown, 2010; see also Souto-Manning, 2011). On the other hand, scepticism remains about the capacity of teacher training programmes to promote social justice when they exhibit the same features as a schooling system 'that is deeply stratified and structured to discriminate between individuals in line with performance hierarchies' (Savage, 2011, p. 33).

Diversity

Like multiculturalism and social justice, diversity is both a fluid label and a contested term in the Australian contemporary polity as well as in Australian pre-service teacher training. It is also inextricably ideological, and thus reflects broader contradictions of competing worldviews, as seen, for example, in its coupling with such concepts as equitable access, quality and social inclusion (Gidley, Hampson, Wheeler, & Bereded-Samuel, 2010). For instance, teacher educators from different countries need to engage with the provocation identified by Gay (2010, p. 143) with regard to 'an aspect of teacher education for diversity that is frequently mentioned but not developed in sufficient detail', which 'is preservice teachers' and teacher educators' attitudes and beliefs about racial, cultural, and ethnic differences'.

Gale and Densmore (2003, p. 107) presented one more optimistic response to this provocation by proposing that 'The challenge for education systems today of increasing diversity presents opportunities for developing democratic dimensions of public education'. Equally optimistically, Mills and Ballantyne (2010, p. 447) posited that it is possible, given sufficient curriculum time, for teacher training programmes to initiate and nurture the hierarchical development of pre-service teachers' dispositions for embracing sociocultural diversity, moving from 'self-awareness/self-reflectiveness' to 'openness' to a 'commitment to social justice'. Similarly, Joseph and Southcott (2009) contended that pre-service teacher training music courses can contribute positively to enhancing understandings of diversity and multiculturalism in Australia, while Kamp and Mansouri (2010, p. 733), based on their research in Melbourne, championed a multidimensional model to manage cultural diversity in Australian schools, 'one that provides the tools for transformative practices to be undertaken to effect positive change in school environments for the benefit of all students'. Likewise in Western Sydney the Refugee Action Support initiative has been effective in helping to prepare pre-service teachers to tutor humanitarian refugee students in local high schools (Ferfolja, 2009).

At the same time, it is timely to acknowledge that, like the Australian higher education sector as a whole (Goedegebuure, Coates, van der Lee, & Meek, 2009),

Australian teacher training is not nearly as socioculturally diverse as the broader Australian community, and moreover that there are particular difficulties for minority pre-service teachers in deriving maximum value from their programmes (Han & Singh, 2007). This in turn generates challenges for teacher educators seeking to internationalize their curricula and to enhance global understandings of sociocultural diversity among prospective teachers (Olmedo & Harbon, 2010), with calls for more critical readings of the meanings and impact on diversity of terms such as 'place', 'identity' and 'community' (McInerney, Smyth, & Down, 2011). Furthermore, it takes time and particular kinds of experiences for teacher graduates to engage effectively in specific contexts of diversity, such as teaching mathematics to Australian Indigenous children in remote locations (Jorgensen [Zevenbergen], Grootenboer, Niesche, & Lerman, 2010; see also Maher, 2012/in press).

These continuing debates and divergences in understandings of the three key concepts of multiculturalism, social justice and diversity outlined here constitute key elements of the landscape for contemporary Australian pre-service teacher training while they also generate considerable challenges and opportunities for it. On the one hand, there are clearly ongoing efforts by Australian teacher educators and their students to engage proactively and productively with identities and pedagogies as they relate to and impact on such markers of difference as ethnicity and gender. On the other hand, equally clearly these efforts must be seen and assessed against the wider backdrop of Australian higher education and even more broadly of Australian society. The tensions – sometimes creative, sometimes counterproductive – between these competing discourses are taken up in greater depth in subsequent chapters.

The book

In this chapter we have introduced the book by presenting contemporary research in the UK, the USA and Australia related to multiculturalism, social justice and diversity, and associated concepts of minority ethnic status and inclusion. This research has been used to highlight both the rationale and the need for this internationally comparative study of identities and pedagogies with regard to pre-service teacher training and its preparation of educators who are willing and able to engage fully with issues of ethnicity and gender.

The remaining chapters in the book portray selected elements of this study. Chapter 1 outlines key debates about identity, specifically through the lenses of 'race', gender and culture, and how they impact on experiences of educational (in)equalities in the UK and Australia. Chapter 2 elaborates crucial dimensions of contemporary theoretical understandings of identity and how those understandings intersect with formal educational provision. Chapter 3 takes further the conceptual and material links between identities and higher education by exploring how identities are manifested differently in different types of British and Australian universities and in relation to policy agenda such as widening participation. Chapter 4 focuses on the enactment of educational identities as they inform and are influenced in turn by the powerful categories of Whiteness and Blackness in both countries. Chapter 5 highlights several methodological and ethical issues encountered in designing and conducting the research into students' experiences and understandings of racialized identities that then forms the basis of Chapter 6, where those experiences and understandings are analysed. Chapter 7 concludes the book by synthesizing the main arguments put forward and distilling their identified strategies for research, policy and practice in pre-service teacher training. The chapter also poses several organizing questions as a way of outlining ideas for creating new and transformative enactments of identity and pedagogy in higher education, in the UK and Australia as well as in other countries.

Note

1	The Training and Development Agency (TDA) is the national agency and recognized sector body that is responsible for the training and development of the school workforce in England. The TDA works in conjunction and partnership with the DfE (Department for Education). The main aims of the TDA are to improve the effectiveness of the school workforce, and to work in partnership with schools to improve the well-being and educational achievement of young people. The TDA was still receiving funding at the time of writing.

Key Debates about Identity, 'Race', Gender and Culture

This chapter provides a discussion and analysis of the key concepts, debates and issues surrounding identity, 'race', gender and culture within the context of higher education in the UK and Australia. It specifically examines the contributions to debates on identity made by Stuart Hall (1991, 1992, 1996), Paul Gilroy (1993) and Avtar Brah (1987, 1996) and more recent interventions by Bhiku Parekh (2006, 2008), Tariq Modood (1992, 1997, 2006), David Gillborn (2008, 2009) and Ann Phoenix (1987) within the UK context. Within the Australian context, the works of Ghassan Hage (2000), Aileen Moreton-Robinson (2004), Andrew Markus (2001; Markus, Jupp, & McDonald, 2009) and others more generally, with recent studies by Dolby (2005) and McLeod and Yates (2006) specifically, have been important.

In this chapter we explore these debates about identity, 'race', gender and culture by presenting a cross-cultural understanding of key issues in relation to identity and pedagogy in higher education in the UK and Australia. The discussion of the concepts, separately and in combination, is grounded in the complex material contexts framing each country that members of minority ethnic communities face each day, and with which teachers, pre-service teachers and teacher educators also need to engage.

The UK context

Within the UK the concept of identity has received considerable attention in the last decade. Issues of identity have been examined in relation to intersectionalities of difference, such as 'race', class and gender. Identity has been analysed in terms of individual positioning in society, both from a micro and a macro level. Much of the writings specifically focused on education have posed the question of how minority ethnic groups continue to be disadvantaged at all levels of their educational careers, from preschool, primary and secondary through to further and higher education.

Identity and 'race'

> I use 'identity' to refer to the meeting point, the point of *suture*, between, on the one hand, the discourses and practices which attempt to 'interpellate', speak to us or hail us into place as the social subjects of particular discourses, and on the other hand, the processes which produce subjectivities, which construct us as subjects which can be 'spoken'. (Hall, 1996, p. 3; *italics in original*)

Identity is – and is likely to remain – a contested concept. There is no one definition of identity, and many writers have attempted to explore this concept in relation to other aspects of belonging and examine what this means in terms of individual and group experiences, whether this is in education, the labour market or society more generally.

The seminal work of Stuart Hall was instrumental when discussing the fluid and slippery concept of identity with regard to 'new ethnicities' (Hall, 1992). Hall (1991) examines how identity itself is constructed through an understanding of the 'other' and indeed the 'outsider' (see Bhopal and Myers, 2008) in which boundaries are created between those who belong and those *who do not*:

> This is the Other that one can only know from the place from which one stands. This is the self as it is inscribed in the gaze of the Other. And this notion which breaks down the boundaries, between outside and inside, between those who belong and those who do not, between those whose histories have been written and those whose histories they have depended on but whose histories cannot be spoken. (Hall, 2000, p. 147)

Gilroy's (1993) work, on the other hand, examines how the notion of culture and resistance is related to the concept of identity. He argues that the idea of a 'Black identity' consists of many shared but also unique practices. There is a complexity associated with the notion of a 'Black identity', one that may have varied yet similar meanings for those who define themselves as such.

More recent understandings of identity have focused on what it means to *choose* an ethnic identity, particularly in relation to those who define themselves as having mixed or dual heritage. Song's (2003) work examines how individuals are able to 'assert and negotiate ethnic identities of their choosing, and the constraints structuring such choices' (p. 1). She argues that choosing an ethnic identity is not necessarily a personal issue; rather it is based on political understandings associated with the negotiation of identity. Furthermore, choosing an ethnic identity may be related to different forms of direct or indirect oppression. Yet at the same time minority people are actively asserting identities – and the meanings associated with such identities – in the public sphere. '. . . these claims to ethnic identity are not only political acts in themselves; they may also be a means of effecting forms of social and political change' (Song, 2003, p. 141). Identity, then, can be understood as 'not a singular but rather a multifaceted and context-specific construct' (Brah, 1996, p. 47).

More recent work on identity by Bhikhu Parekh (2008) explores the 'new politics of identity' and focuses on globalization and its impact on identity in the contemporary world. It is the very process of globalization that can challenge traditional identity in that world. Parekh conceptualizes identity as having three separate but related dimensions:

> . . . the personal, the social and the human. The first identifies an individual as a unique person; the second as a member of a particular group or structure of relationship; and the third as a member of the universal human community. (2008, p. 4)

Identity is of course related to cultural understandings in society. For Parekh, cultural diversity originates from many different sources: 'Many societies include several ethnic, religious, cultural and other communities with more or less distinct bodies of beliefs and practices' (2008, p. 80). Parekh argues that, with the impact of globalization, members of society are exposed to a variety of modes of thought and approaches; consequently they either take these on or oppose them, particularly with regard to religious belief and thought. 'The increasing reassertion of religion further reinforces diversity' (2008, p. 80).

Fredrick Barth's influential historical conceptualization of ethnic boundaries is also relevant here. According to Barth (1969), ethnic groups exist as part of categories of self-identification and ascription by others. In this process, ethnic groups are able to distinguish themselves from others owing to the presence of boundaries that they create between themselves and others. Consequently, ethnic groups are identified by, and identify themselves through, their relationships to boundaries. These ethnic boundaries are identified through particular signifiers – for example, language, history, religion or shared traditions. Ethnicity, then, is a mechanism for boundary formation and boundary maintenance. It is clear who belongs and who *does not*.

Bhopal and Myers (2008) take this notion of boundary formation further to examine how the 'other' and the 'outsider' remain on the boundaries as they are identified as 'strangers'. They use the work of Simmel (1950) and Bauman (1991) to understand how the position of the 'other' is marked out:

> Whether or not boundaries are created by insiders or outsiders, they constitute a notion of difference between both parties. Boundary formation and boundary maintenance are inextricably linked to a labelling process in which the upper hand lies with the more powerful dominant society. (Bhopal & Myers, 2008, p. 106)

Boundaries thus mark out a sense of belonging and a sense of who is considered the 'other'. In the same vein, more recent work by Bhopal (2010) has examined how women from minority ethnic backgrounds, particularly British-born third generation women, engage in communities of practice in higher education to find security and safety in a world in which they continue to experience racism and marginalization (please see below for a more detailed discussion of this issue).

A number of researchers have examined the concept of identity in relation to multiculturalism. Modood (1992) states, '. . . multiculturalism must rest on an affirmation of shared moral certainties: it cannot just be about differences' (p. 4). He argues that, if we ask people to assimilate when there is overt racial discrimination in society, such an approach runs the risk of greater conflict and destabilization in that society. This would further result in 'the fragmentation of communities that are currently the sources of stability, group pride and self esteem' (p. 5). He encourages the use of a 'hyphenated nationality' that is quite often used in the USA where citizens describe themselves as 'Black-American' or 'African-American'. He contends that this assertion of one's ethnic identity within a recognition of one's nationality encourages different forms of ethnicity but does not challenge the ties that signify nationhood and citizenship.

Modood (1997) suggests that there are two views of the conceptualization of citizenship and what that means in terms of equality and multiculturalism. These are 'the right to assimilate to the majority/dominant culture in the public sphere and the toleration of "difference" in the private sphere and the right to one's "difference" (minority, ethnicity) recognized and supported in the public and private spheres' (p. 20). Multiculturalism is one way forward in the recognition of difference and diversity in relation to educational experiences and multiple identities. Furthermore, with regard to education, Modood (1997) argues that education policy should recognize difference by creating positive attitudes towards what multiculturalism is and how it can be practised in the classroom.

Parekh (2006), on the other hand, examines multiculturalism through the discourses of cultural diversity and culturally embedded differences. Parekh argues that identity (in relation to multiculturalism in particular) is a contested term:

> Although the term identity is sometimes inflated to cover almost everything that characterizes an individual or group, most advocates of these movements use it to refer to those chosen or inherited characteristics that define them as certain kinds of persons or groups and form an integral part of their self-understanding. (p. 1)

'Race', class and gender

The phenomenon of identity has long been associated with intersectionalities of difference. It was the work of influential Black Feminists such as Hazel Carby, bell hooks, Patricia Hill Collins and others that introduced the concept of 'race' and its influence on identity and oppression for women from minority ethnic backgrounds (Brah, 1987; Carby, 1982; Hill Collins, 1990; hooks, 1984; Phoenix, 1987). Black women began to question the meaning of Feminism and its application to the lives of non-White women. Many argued for the need to understand the diverse histories of minority women such as slavery, colonialism and imperialism and the impact of such experiences on women's lives, particularly in relation to what Feminism meant and what it was trying to achieve and *for whom*.

Against this backdrop, Avtar Brah's work was particularly important in the UK as it explored the lives and experiences of Black African-Caribbean and British Asian women with an emphasis on examining intersectionalities of difference in relation to 'race', class and gender. Research identified how Black and Asian women's experiences in education and the labour market, regardless of their class position, will always be affected by their experiences of racism (Bhopal, 2010; Brah, 1996). Their visible difference will always affect their position in society, one nearly always of disadvantage compared to that of White women. According to Brah, this notion of difference '. . . may be construed as a *social relation* constructed within systems of power underlying structures of class, racism, gender, sexuality, and so on' (1996, p. 88; *italics in original*).

In using the concept of diaspora, Brah (1996) was able to analyse how power differentiates identities and also how power can situate different diasporas in relation to one another. Based on this analysis, Brah introduced the concept of 'diaspora space':

> Diaspora space is the point at which boundaries of inclusion and exclusion, of belonging and otherness, of 'us' and 'them', are contested. My argument is that diaspora space as a conceptual category is 'inhabited', not only by those who have migrated and their descendants, but equally by those who are constructed and represented as indigenous. (Brah, 1996, p. 205)

Here the focus is on an understanding of intersectionalities of difference, but also on being aware that diaspora space is *affected* by intersectionalities and quite often can be *defined* by them.

More recent work has explored how intersectionalities of difference are located within the lived realities of women's lives and how these intersectionalities have a direct influence on the achievements of minority ethnic women. Mirza (2009) explores the use of an 'embodied intersectionality' to '. . . demonstrate the processes of "being and becoming" a gendered and raced subject of academic and educational discourse' (pp. 3–4). She argues that intersections of 'race' and gender are crucial in understanding the educational experiences of minority ethnic women in society today. 'Black cultures of resistance' used by women are key in understanding their experiences in education. Furthermore, she outlines how many of the myths associated with Black underachievement are related to aspects of racism and everyday stereotypes associated with what it means to be a 'Black woman' in British society.

Many researchers have begun to explore intersectionalities of difference and what this can tell us about the diversity of experiences and identities. The pioneering work of Crenshaw (1989, 1991) addressed the concept and analysis of intersectionality. Her work in the USA was a critical response to the silence of Feminism in addressing the needs of African-American women and their oppression. Crenshaw's work focuses on the recognition that oppression exists through multiple axes, with each individual axis interacting with and affecting the others: 'Black women can experience discrimination in any number of ways and that contradiction arises from assumptions that their claims of inclusion must be interactional. Consider an analogy to traffic in an intersection, coming and going in all four directions' (1989, pp. 321–2). Collins (2005) has further argued that intersectional paradigms of difference focus on power relations in which individuals have different levels of power and occupy different positions within the multiple axes of social hierarchy (see also Siedman, 1974).

Other scholars have argued that to examine intersectionality it is crucial to explore the various facets of identity in relation to a crystal (Richardson, 2000) or even a 'faceted crystal' (Sims, 2009). Tracy and Trethway link this to power discourses: 'By conceiving of identities as ongoing, emergent and not entirely predictable crystals, people are forced to acknowledge a range of possible selves embodied in a range of contexts – even as they are constrained by discourses of power' (2005, p. 189).

Post-structuralists have also studied the concept of intersectionality, but do so by exploring the concept of 'agency'. This has resulted in an analysis of what difference means and how it can be understood (Butler, 1990; Spivak, 1999), and has led to the development of postcolonial studies and postcolonial Feminism, particularly through a Foucauldian or Derridean discourse. Such approaches have been developed into 'border theory' (Lewis, 2000) or an understanding of 'diaspora' or 'diaspora space' (Brah, 1996), as discussed above. More recently, Brah and Phoenix have argued that '. . . social class (and its intersections with gender and "race" or sexuality) are simultaneously subjective, structural and about social positioning and everyday practices' (2004, p. 75).

Floya Anthias takes the concept of intersectionality one step further and uses the concept of 'translocational positionality' to address some of the difficulties associated with the concept. Translocational positionality '. . . addresses issues of identity in terms of locations which are not fixed but are context, meaning and time related and which therefore involve shifts and contradictions. It thereby provides an intersectional framing for the understanding of belonging' (2008, p. 5). She pays particular attention to social locations and processes and how these are linked to the fragmentation of contemporary life where belonging is signified by borders and boundaries. Differences then are conceptualized as a set of processes that can be both material and cultural.

McCall (2005), on the other hand, has argued that the study of intersectionality has introduced new methodological problems and has limited the range of methodological approaches that can be used to study it. In her own work, she uses three different approaches to the analysis of intersectionality: the anticategorical complexity; the intracategorical complexity; and the intercategorical complexity. She defines intersectionality as '. . . the relationships among multiple dimensions and modalities of social relations and subject formations' (2005, p. 1771). Her approach analyses power and knowledge through the mechanisms of exclusion and inclusion. What is clear from these works is that the study of intersectionality has identified novel ways of understanding the concept of identities and belonging in contemporary society.

Culture

Culture is also a 'fuzzy' term, one that has varied meanings in different contexts. Accordingly there are many competing definitions of culture. Brah states, 'Culture may be viewed as the symbolic construction of the vast array of a social group's life experiences. Culture is the embodiment, the chronicle of a group's history' (1996, p. 18). Culture, then, like identity is dynamic, constantly changing and evolving. Cultures can change and adapt at any given time and at any given place. Cultures can and do evolve throughout different historical periods.

Brah goes on to state, 'At any given time a group will inherit certain cultural institutions and traditions, but its acts of reiteration or repudiation, its everyday interactions and its ritual practices will serve to select, modify, and transform these institutions' (1996, p. 18). Again like identity, cultures can be similar, yet different. At some points in history cultures may be very similar, yet also retain their individual differences. As Brah notes, 'Cultural differences, however, are rarely the outcome of a simple process of differentiation. Rather, this "difference" is constituted within the intersections of socio-political and economic relations' (p. 19). In order to analyse culture, it is important to discuss how power relations play a part in how culture itself is understood.

Inequality and education in the UK: 'Race', class and gender

Much of the literature that has focused on the effects of 'race', class and gender on the educational experiences of minority ethnic groups has examined the myth of underachievement for Black women (Mirza, 1992), the so-called cultural problems associated with Asian girls and reasons why they may not pursue higher education (Basit, 1995) as well as the racism experienced by minority ethnic groups at all levels of their educational careers (Bhopal, 2008; DfES, 2007; Gillborn, 2008; Skelton et al., 2007). Furthermore, research has argued that highlighting 'underachievement' detracts from an analysis of the failure of the education system itself (Mirza, 1992). What is more, some groups who may be failing nationally are in fact succeeding in local areas and individual schools (Gillborn & Gipps, 1996). 'Race' is shown to have a huge influence on the achievements of African-Caribbean and Asian groups at all levels in the education system. These groups are then compared against one another from which a 'hierarchy of achievement' results, with some groups doing better than others. For example, Indian groups are said to be achieving the same levels of success at higher education as their White counterparts, whereas Black Caribbean groups are performing the worst (Stevenson & Lang, 2010).

A great deal of research has examined the relationship between social class background and educational achievement (Reay et al., 2001; Stevenson & Lang, 2010). The research generally reveals that the higher the social class background, the higher the educational achievement (at all levels). Generally speaking, however, social class as a concept is difficult to measure and it is usually associated with whether a child is eligible for free school meals. When 'race' is taken into account, research has shown that social class and 'race' have a significant impact on educational achievement (Gillborn & Gipps, 1996; Gillborn & Mirza, 2000; Gillborn & Youdell, 2000). However, when class differences are taken into account differences in achievement are shown to be due to ethnic background (Denmack et al., 2000). The data suggest that inequalities in education persist and in some cases particular groups have not shown an increase in levels of achievement and attainment (Denmack et al., 2000). Mirza suggests,

> In the context of an inclusive educational agenda that seeks to raise standards for all, this evidence indicates a need for clarity and guidance in translating the commitment to equality and inclusion (so often expressed at the national level) into policy proposals and practice at the local/school level. (2009, p. 39)

Quite often, even though the data reveal low levels of educational achievement for some minority ethnic groups, in reality the policy discourses do little to tackle these problems head on, which would make a difference to the educational experiences of those groups who remain poorly represented in formal education.

Recent research by Gillborn (2008) has demonstrated the persistent 'race' inequalities in education:

> Contrary to the popular image created by media scare stories and official Gap Talk, particular minoritized groups (Black students and their peers of Pakistani and Bangladeshi heritage) continue to be significantly less likely to achieve the key benchmarks when compared with White peers of the same gender. (2008, p. 69)

Education policy-making has played a key role in creating and sustaining these inequalities and does little to improve the chances of greater success for those groups who remain marginalized in formal education. 'The overwhelming weight of social and educational policy, therefore, has failed to address race equality: it has pandered to White racist sentiment and left the principal race inequalities untouched' (Gillborn, 2008, p. 89). Gillborn notes that the existence of White Supremacy in education is an example of how educational inequalities are legitimated by the interests of dominant White society.

The experiences of minority ethnic students in higher education in England are complex. Much of the research seems to suggest that minority ethnic students are more likely to attend 'new' (post-1992) universities than the traditional 'red brick' universities (Bhopal, 2010; Modood & Shiner, 2002). Furthermore, parents' social class (Reay et al., 2005) and 'race' (Modood, 2006) have a significant impact on which universities and courses students choose. The overall picture in the last decade shows some change in terms of increasing participation in higher education for students from minority ethnic backgrounds. This picture, however, is complex, with some groups still lagging behind in higher education, such as those from Bangladeshi and Pakistani backgrounds (see Bhopal, 2010). Research has shown that minority ethnic students prefer to attend universities where there is a large intake of minority ethnic students (Reay et al., 2005), which is also linked to a 'critical mass' of similar students where localism is favoured (Bhopal, 2010).

Much of the research does point out the continued racism and marginalization faced by some students when they attend university (Bhopal, 2010). This seems to be the case more so for those from Muslim backgrounds (Bagguley & Hussain, 2007; Federation of Islamic Studies, 2005). This in itself may be related to the bombings in London on 7 July 2005 in which the bombers were from British Muslim backgrounds, which sparked further unrest and uncertainty regarding the position of Muslim men in the UK, particularly in relation to the 'war on terror'. However, despite the difficulties that some minority ethnic students face when attending university, recent research has shown how some groups, particularly Asian women, use their support networks to engage in 'communities of practice' in which they find security and safety in an otherwise insecure environment (Bhopal, 2010). Many Asian women are able to overcome the barriers that they face in higher education to achieve the success that they need to enter the labour market to ensure that they are able to be employed in professional and managerial occupations; hence formal education is a route to increased social mobility.

More recent research has indicated that higher education in the UK is now at a crisis point, with many students from diverse backgrounds having paid higher fees than their pervious counterparts and hence leaving higher education with record levels of debt and with no jobs (Ainley & Allen, 2010). This may be further highlighted by the introduction of student fees. On 3 November 2010, the new Coalition Government (Conservatives and Liberal Democrats) in the UK laid out plans for a reform of university funding that includes an increase in tuition fees payable by home and international students. These changes came into effect for the start of the 2012 academic year.

The introduction of student fees sparked opposition from student groups, which resulted in demonstrations and riots in London. Consequently, the numbers of students applying for university places in 2011 showed a dramatic increase. Applications for university places soared by 2.5%, according to figures published by the UK Universities and Colleges Admissions Service (December 2010, UCAS website www.ucas.co.uk/about_us/media_enquiries/media_releases/2011/040111). Over 8000 more students applied compared to the numbers who had applied at the same point in the previous year.

This section of the chapter has explored the research on key debates around the concepts of identity, belonging and difference from a UK perspective. The following section examines equivalent research from the Australian perspective.

The Australian context

Like their UK counterparts, Australian researchers from several disciplinary backgrounds have engaged comprehensively with the concept of identity and its connections with 'race' (also interpreted as ethnicity), gender, culture and class. The resulting scholarship has highlighted how complex, diverse, fluid and multifaceted that concept and those connections are, leading to similar challenges for educators and educational researchers seeking to understand existing experiences and structures and striving to make them more positive and transformative where appropriate and possible. From this perspective, the links between formal education and particular dimensions of identity are enduringly significant and worthy of ongoing analysis and evaluation (see for example Blackmore, 2010; Pini, Price, & McDonald, 2010; Ramzan, Pini, & Bryant, 2009).

Identity and 'race'

Evidence abounds in the Australian literature of the continuing connections among identity, 'race' and formal education. This is certainly the case for minority ethnic communities who experience particular forms of racism and educational disadvantage, such as female and male Arab-Australian school students (Mansouri & Trembath, 2005), members of ethnically diverse schools in south-western Sydney (Reid & Young, 2012/forthcoming) and western Melbourne (Bowden & Doughney, 2010), and Chinese international students completing doctorates in Australia (Singh, 2009). This is despite the finding that working with ethnically diverse students impacts positively on university students' learning and their preparation for entering a diverse workforce (Denson & Zhang, 2010).

A crucial element of the scholarship related to identity in both Australia and the UK is the proposition that the formal education system is a racialized, gendered and class-based phenomenon (see for example Matthews, 2008; Phoenix, 2009; Shore, 2010) that is predisposed and even hard wired to promote the interests of the majority and mainstream culture. This is clearly a complex argument that draws on diverse strands of thought from such paradigms as critical theory, postcolonialism and post-structuralism and that attributes this phenomenon to forces like neoliberalism (Kamp & Mansouri, 2010) and the continuing effects of colonialism (Gulson & Parkes, 2009). This and the subsequent chapters in this book are intended to illustrate selected aspects of this argument, while also identifying strategies that have been demonstrated as being effective in engaging with the argument and helping to ameliorate some of its negative manifestations.

This complex interplay between identity and 'race' within the contexts of formal education in Australia has been taken up by several researchers, deploying a wide range of research paradigms, methods and questions. For instance, McLeod and Yates (2006) trace the changes in the lives of 26 Australian adolescents and their development of their selves and their subjectivities in a longitudinal study against the backdrop of so-called New Times and through the lenses of 'race', class and gender vis-à-vis schooling provision. Their analysis is differentiated and multifaceted – for example, they acknowledge that the growth of a racialized identity resulting from the nexus between processes of schooling and of subjectivity exhibits institutional and national specificities, differing from one school to others in the study and also differing between Australia and other countries. Their finding that 'The effects of different school cultures are also evident in how students articulate their political values' (p. 11) is significant because it highlights that individual school settings can and do make a difference to how broader social forces such as racism and sexism are manifested and mediated.

Certainly the theme of national differences in experiences of racialized identities and consequently in dispositions for engaging with the challenges and opportunities of the 'global imagination' is taken up by Dolby (2005) in her comparison between Australian and US undergraduates' reflections on studying abroad. Dolby contends that 'American students' strong national identity often prevents them from exploring the possibilities of global affiliation' (p. 101), and that 'Australian students' relatively weak national identity allows for a robust global sense of place, but is sometimes constrained by a limited tolerance for racial and ethnic diversity' (p. 101). We are less concerned with the content of these generalizations than with their underlying assumption, which is that sense of identity, however and wherever it is constructed, exercises a powerful impact on how individuals and groups see themselves and others against the backdrop of the wider world. Moreover, the elements of that sense of identity vary widely in space and time, within as well as across the participating members of constituent communities. This point is fundamental, not only for understanding how closely and strongly identity and 'race' are intertwined, but also for helping to create new and viable alternatives to less positive aspects of that interdependence.

Another approach to this parallel project of theorizing and practicing multiple kinds of racialized identities is exhibited by Ghassan Hage in his well-known book analysing Australia in the late 1990s, *White nation: Fantasies of White supremacy in a multicultural society* (2000). Hage sees this nexus between theory and practice as crucial, and urges the importance of 'establishing the way in which the racist classifications of the powerful distinguish themselves from other racist classifications and reveal themselves to be forms of *empowered practical prejudice*' (p. 36; *italics in original*). Much of the analysis of the interviews reported in the book relates to different kinds of vividly named constructed identities, such as 'the homely imaginary of nationalist practices' (p. 38), 'the imaginary of the nationalist manager and the other as object' (p. 42), 'from citizenship to practical nationality' (p. 49) and 'guardians of the national order: the field of whiteness and the white national aristocracy' (p. 55). On the basis of that analysis, Hage articulates the notion of 'a White ideal, [which] like all capital, is not only something to be accumulated, but it is also an historical construct and an object of struggle over its content' (p. 59). This comparison with capital again highlights the economic and political dimensions of racialized identities and also reinforces widely divergent levels of such capital held by different members of the same nation or society.

The collection of articles that constitute *Whitening race: Essays in social and cultural criticism* (Moreton-Robinson, 2004) takes Hage's (2000) concept of 'a White ideal' in a number of specific directions. For instance, there are elaborations of 'the way whiteness erupts in the psycho-social and ontological realms of subjectivity to reproduce colonising relations in different contexts' (p. 1), of the complex connections among 'subjectivity, whiteness and ways of knowing' (p. 2) and of how 'whiteness and race . . . shape ways of knowing, acting and producing knowledge' (p. 2), and of 'issues of whiteness and subjectivity, as constituted through various disciplinary knowledges' (p. 2). Another example is the ways in which White racialized identities are constituted by means of denying and devaluing other types of racialized identities:

> . . . the cultural pluralist understanding of multiculturalism works in Australia, as a weak form of assimilation. . . . Needless to say, this is not a practice which respects the integrity of the Other – the Other which . . . in a general sense has been produced as Other through the very characteristic of the border as a characteristic feature of modernity. (Stratton, 2004, p. 238)

All of this highlights the profoundly politicized character of racialized identities. Furthermore, it illustrates how that politicized character assumes particular forms in response to specific contemporary political forces and influences. For instance, Markus (2001) draws attention to the following examples of the politicized underpinnings of racialized identities:

> . . . the battle which takes place over definitions and the political significance of their outcomes; the core ideas of racial thought and their varying manifestations; the currently dominant form of culturalist racism to be found in western societies; and the need to distinguish between form and substance in evaluation of political argument. (p. 3)

While Markus's (2001) book *Race: John Howard and the remaking of Australia* is concerned with the politicization of discourses and policies related to ethnic diversity under the former Australian conservative prime minister John Howard, he acknowledges that such discourses and policies have been politicized under prime ministers of varying political persuasion. For example, with regard to the Australian Labor prime minister Gough Whitlam, 'The Whitlam years were, however, stronger on rhetoric than achievement in the development of multicultural policy, . . .' (p. 26). Similarly, Markus's book with James Jupp and

Peter McDonald (2009), *Australia's immigration revolution*, written during the prime ministership of Kevin Rudd, Howard's Labour successor, highlights the complexities of managing immigration policy at a time of recession and the accelerating growth of a global labour market in certain occupations.

In common with all other nations in the world, Australia has exhibited, through its historical developments and its contemporary enactments, the continuing complexity of its interplay between multiple manifestations of identities and 'race'. That interplay reinforces the contentious character of these manifestations – that they are contested and debated, rather than accepted and settled. This contentious character derives from the economic and political underpinnings of the debate, and the key point that racialized constructions of identity always seem to yield winners and losers instead of equity within diversity. This point generates all kinds of consequences with long-term significance, not least for pre- and in-service teachers and the teacher educators who work with them to understand and contribute to this debate.

'Race', class and gender

As with the UK, so too with Australia: the proposition of the intersectionalities of difference has resulted in several rich analyses of contemporary identity constructions and manifestations, including the connections among 'race', class and gender. These analyses have reinforced the fluid, multiple and politicized character of identities, and have demonstrated how they are strongly influenced by broader cultural, political and sociocultural forces, and how strongly in turn they influence the perceptions and actions of individuals, groups and communities.

One of the principal theoretical strengths afforded by adopting an intersectionalities approach to understanding identities is that it helps to avoid the conceptual dead end represented by binary thinking (see also Midgley, Tyler, Danaher, & Mander, 2011). As Naples (2008) remarks:

> Regardless of whether one takes an embodied, relational, structural or epistemological approach to intersectional analysis, an intersectional angle of vision inevitably highlights the limits of dichotomous formulations and borders between: us–them, oppressor–oppressed, western–non-western, local–global, activism–scholarship and theory–practice. (p. 2)

Naples (2008) contends that what she calls 'intersectional feminist praxis' (p. 3), which brings together theoretical and practical experiences and understandings of fundamental identity markers like gender, has a key role to play in disrupting often unhelpful boundaries:

> . . . intersectional feminist praxis provides a valuable framework for cross-border activism of many different kinds, including crossing the borders between academic disciplines, academic feminism and feminist activism. Borders are undeniably human made; therefore we must continue to ask who has the ability to construct borders, what functions do different borders serve, who are privileged by different kinds of borders, . . . (p. 12)

This linking between identities understood in terms of fluidity, hybridity, mobility and multiplicity on the one hand and efforts to challenge and unsettle identity constituents that are inequitable and marginalizing on the other is a major theme of this book and a crucial element of more enabling and transformative approaches to identities and pedagogies in higher education, not only in the UK and Australia but in other countries as well.

As an elaboration of this proposition, Santoro, Reid, Crawford and Simpson (2012) present the example of Indigenous Australian teachers, who embody and mobilize multiple identities through their personal and public lives:

> The participants in the study reported here are teachers – they are also Indigenous. As we argue, an 'Indigenous teacher' identity can be, and is often, ascribed by others, and understood as fixed and singular. The ascription of an essentialised identity disregards the complexities within and between the category 'Indigenous', as well as the category 'teacher'. There are multiple ways of being both Indigenous and teacher that are shaped by social and discursive practices, as well as factors such as gender and social class. Furthermore, such factors are inextricably intertwined and intersect in complex ways. Indigenous teachers, for example, are also gendered, and they are positioned and take up positionings within social classes. (p. 257)

Moreover, 'Identities are always being produced, in a state of becoming, changing and shifting in response to different social contexts and dynamics' (Santoro, Reid, Crawford, & Simpson, 2012, p. 257). In addition, 'Indigenous teachers "become" who they are, as they construct and perform themselves in the range of social situations in which they participate' (p. 258). Identities understood as being constructed and performed are very different from conceptualizing them as essentialized, fixed and singular.

As another example of intersectionalities informing Australian identities, Couch's (2011) analysis of the complex phenomenon of homelessness among

Australian young refugees draws on this concept: 'An intersectional analysis directs attention away from an exclusive focus on individual stories and experiences, to consideration of larger systemic and structural inequalities' (p. 44). Those inequalities relate not only to the usual identity categories such as ethnicity, class and gender but also more specific markers like family relationships, mental and emotional health, and learning difficulties. The result is often mutual misunderstandings, with refugee young people sometimes not being aware of the availability of relevant services and service providers sometimes holding stereotypical views of refugee young people.

The conceptual insights provided by the notion of intersectionalities of difference can also yield practical strategies with the potential to ameliorate – at least to some degree – these kinds of inequalities:

> … though theory is a few steps ahead of practice, awareness of intersectionality is slowly but surely affecting domains such as human rights advocacy, identity politics, and social movements . . ., counseling, psychotherapy, and social work . . ., and workplace diversity training. (Gopaldas & Fischer, 2012, p. 394)

For instance, Clausen and Anderson (2012) posit intercultural playtexts as an effective postcolonial pedagogical device for teaching about Indigenous Australian issues to non-Indigenous senior secondary drama students. This device is based on four 'Principles for intercultural work' (p. 183):

- 'Challenging mediated representations of Indigenous Australians' (p. 183)
- 'Questions about cultural identity' (p. 184)
- 'Race and racism' (p. 185)
- 'The power of intersubjectivity' (p. 185).

On the basis of their experiences and analysis, Clausen and Anderson (2012) articulate the reasons for what they perceive as the effectiveness of the strategy:

> The success of this performance task for these students was made possible through a foundation of prior learning experiences that encouraged an engagement with culturally unfamiliar experiences and perspectives that resonated with the participants in both an intellectual and [an] emotional way. The richness of the learning activities created a space in which the students could reflect on their own cultural identity in light of the historical, social and political backdrop of White and Indigenous relations in Australia. It is clear that learning that incorporates the kinaesthetic expression of an intercultural playtext encourages transformational learning. By encouraging

the dynamic between thinking and feeling, teachers can create changes in understanding, increased self-awareness, reflection, imagination, enthusiasm, intelligent caring and a commitment to the well being of self and others. A highly desirable outcome if we wish to contribute to the development of active and informed citizens who are able to relate to and communicate across cultures. (pp. 188–9)

At the same time, it is important to note that none of these features of the strategy is a guarantee of its success, and that the same approach could be taken in different educational contexts with less effective outcomes. This timely reminder derives not only from the inherent complexity and unpredictability of educational settings but also from the even greater complexity and unpredictability of intersectionalities of difference.

Culture

Like the UK literature, Australian scholarship highlights culture as a dynamic, fluid and multifaceted concept and phenomenon. These characteristics certainly animate contemporary debates about issues ranging from the intercultural dimension of internationalization in Australian higher education (Crichton & Scarino, 2007) to competing discourses of cosmopolitanness and otherness in Australian sociological imaginaries (Calcutt, Woodward, & Skrbis, 2009) to the place of otherness in essentialist understandings of 'Indigenous culture' framing some approaches to Indigenous Australian cultural training for health workers (Downing & Kowal, 2011, p. 5) to the intersection between difference and racialization in the experiences of China-educated nurses working in Australia (Zhou, Windsor, Theobald, & Coyer, 2011) to the role of the cultural in conceptualizing contemporary learning experiences (Billett, 2009).

All of this highlights culture as a fluid, shifting and even slippery concept with widely divergent meanings in Australian scholarship reflecting equally divergent disciplinary and ideological positions. From one perspective, despite the assumption of culturally pluralist values, some seemingly multicultural children's literature can actually function as the site of assimilationist views of culture (Yoon, Simpson, & Haag, 2010). By contrast, when aligned with a critically informed approach, education about culture can contribute positively to assisting Australian health-care professionals to reduce racism in their interactions with Indigenous Australian (Durey, 2010). Between these two standpoints lie ongoing – and sometimes acrimonious – debates about 'the key interlinking issues of authenticity, identity, and culture' (Wohling, 2009, p. 6) and about 'what constitutes authentic and inauthentic culture and which group or individual possesses an authentic culture and knowledge' (p. 8) among Indigenous Australian communities. As with other aspects of identities, culture is often politicized and appropriated by proponents of particular ideologies to progress their interests and potentially to critique the ideologies of others.

Inequality and education in Australia: 'Race', class and gender

One of the key debates continuing to confront teachers, teacher educators and educational researchers alike is the extent to which formal education is complicit with strategies of racialized, class-based and gendered marginalization whose effect is to perpetuate educational inequalities. This debate is encapsulated in Windle's (2008) analysis of the post-compulsory schooling experiences of second-generation Turkish-background students in Australia. On the one hand, '. . . gender and ethnicity organise, make legible and obscure the production of educational disadvantage in these sites' (p. 157). On the other hand, without disavowing the need for appropriate accompanying resources, there are potential grounds for helping to challenge that disadvantage based on '. . . high levels of student optimism . . .' and '. . . strong confidence and faith in schools amongst students...' (p. 157). It is the tension and struggle between these opposing positions that are evident in much contemporary Australian education scholarship. Or as Tyler (2011) expresses it even more succinctly: 'Within every classroom there exists the potential for inequality in various forms. It is essential to recognise the role of the educator in either the reproduction or [the] transformation of these potential inequalities' (p. 21).

With regard to the racialized dimension of this debate, a variety of experiences and perspectives is discernible in the Australian literature. Lea, Thompson, McRae-Williams and Wegner (2011) explicate what could be interpreted variously as resigned acceptance of, and/or enraged despair about, a yawning chasm between educational policy and practice related to renewed efforts to promote the 'engagement' of Indigenous Australians in northern Australia:

> In its homogenisation of Indigenous issues, reification of cultural distinction and foregrounding of disengagement as an issue, Australian education policy is also about non-engagement, in that it excludes key issues from policy consideration while appearing to be inclusive. The education sector does not systematically engage with the grinding issues that Indigenous families face

in their everyday worlds; and since Indigenous people do not really expect
schools to know how to solve their issues, the call for engagement and its
resolution [are] perfectly irresolvable. (p. 321)

Standing in stark contrast to this disjuncture between educational policy and
practice is a longitudinal study, assertively entitled 'Cultural diversity as an
educational advantage', of the management of cultural diversity by a group of
Arab-Australian secondary students and their families (Mansouri, 2007). This
study found that 'key pedagogical initiatives and community–school partnership
initiatives . . . have been collaborative developed to effect positive change in the
multifaceted schooling experience' (p. 15).

In terms of the class-based dimension of this debate, that dimension is
articulated as '. . . the ways in which class advantage and disadvantage are
emotionally inscribed and embodied in educational settings' (Pini, Price, &
McDonald, 2010, p. 17). Yet this issue is complicated by its intersections with other
markers of difference in Australian education; for example, '. . . moral ascriptions
of class by the teachers are powerfully shaped by dominant socio-cultural
constructions of rurality that equate "the rural" with agriculture' (p. 17). It is
also framed by continuing argument about the character of class and whether
it should be retained or jettisoned as a means of explaining socioeconomic
inequality in educational settings (Theobald, 2011). Certainly there has long been
a recognition by successive Australian governments of the need to implement
strategies focused directly on making higher education more accessible and
appealing to variously disadvantaged students, although the effectiveness and
impact of those strategies remain unclear (Carson, 2009).

In relation to the gendered character of educational inequalities in Australia
today, there is also evidence of widespread debate. For instance, drawing on
modernization theory and based on nationally representative survey data
between 1965 and 2005, Marks (2009b) states baldly, 'Gender inequalities in
education have been reversed, and the gender gap in earnings has declined' (p.
917). Yet, against the backdrop of these broader trends, certain communities in
Australia experience very different opportunities and outcomes. For instance,
'. . . there are significant gendered barriers to educational participation among
members of the Sudanese refugee groups' (Hatoss & Huijser, 2010, p. 147), and
more widely '. . . women from refugee backgrounds are particularly at risk and
face cultural and linguistic barriers in accessing educational opportunities' (p.
147). Furthermore, competing constructions of masculinity have been argued
as having particular significance for some boys in Australian schools (Connell,

2008). Moreover, changing approaches to educational governance have been linked with alternative understandings of and enactments of gender equity in education in Australia (Blackmore, 2011).

Thus the racialized, class-based and gendered dimensions of inequalities and their associations or otherwise with educational policies and provision lie at the centre of ongoing debates within Australian scholarship. These debates are complex and diverse, and are connected with broader disjunctures among competing scholarly disciplines and research paradigms. According to these multiple perspectives, education emerges as a vehicle for individual and communal sociocultural transformation, as politically innocent and neutral, or as complicit with the forces of marginalization – and sometimes as all three.

This chapter has elaborated several contemporary debates about 'race', gender and culture and what they might mean for understandings of identities and pedagogies in higher education in the UK and Australia. The terms of these debates are contentious and divergent, and are also sometimes politicized and seemingly appropriated by particular interest groups. It is difficult but crucial for teachers and teacher educators to understand these debates and to develop publicly and privately defensible positions in relation to them if they are to discharge their multiple roles and responsibilities effectively and ethically.

Theoretical Understandings of Identity

This chapter elaborates crucial dimensions of contemporary theoretical understandings of identity and how those understandings intersect with formal educational provision – specifically teaching training in the UK and Australia. It explores the positioning of students within the academy and how this is affected by gender, 'race', class and power. It draws on selected empirical research to examine how identities of Whiteness and Blackness are translated within the context of higher education. It also begins to investigate how students understand their own identities within this context and how those identities are understood within the space of higher education.

The UK context

In the UK, there is no legal requirement for primary or secondary Postgraduate Certificate in Education (PGCE) students to complete compulsory courses on the teaching of 'race', racism, diversity and inclusion, or how to deal specifically with incidents of racism in the classroom. ITE providers are expected to adhere to guidance provided by the Department for Education (DfE) and legal frameworks (such as the Race Relations Amendment Act 2000). From this perspective, ITE providers have to be aware of the legal framework that exists around 'race', diversity and inclusion and what is meant by these terms. However, this can be interpreted in different ways, and the emphasis on these issues depends on the respective ITE provider and the schools where teacher trainees carry out their placements. In relation to these issues, previous research has found that, when students are asked to examine copies of Equality Policies, many find that schools simply do not know about them, do not have them to hand and suggest that they are somewhere in the school, which indicates that such policies are adhering to a tick box exercise in which having the policies is simply not enough (see Bhopal, Harris, & Rhamie, 2009).

Qualified Teacher Status (QTS)

All trainee teachers have to be awarded Qualified Teacher Status (QTS) before they can teach in a classroom. The standards for the award of QTS are set by the TDA. In order for teachers to be awarded QTS, they must meet specific outcome statements; these were developed through a consultation process in conjunction with the TDA and other professional bodies for teachers to achieve advanced and excellent teaching standards. A number of stakeholders were involved in the consultation process that contributed to the development of the QTS standards. The consultation was based on the implementation of the *Every Child Matters Agenda* as well as equality duties and workforce reform. The QTS standards have to be met by all trainee teachers if they want to qualify for QTS, whether this is through the PGCE or otherwise. The standards are important because they enable the ITT providers to have autonomy in how they organize their teacher training in their respective institutions and how they will in turn respond to the needs of individual trainee teachers. However, the TDA does not set a specified curriculum for ITT providers and they do not specify how the training should be designed or managed. The QTS standards enable ITT providers to have increased flexibility in how they design their teacher training programmes. Many of the standards that are set are related to obtaining the highest degree of excellence and professionalism in the assessment of trainees to achieve their QTS. The trainees have to provide evidence through assessment that they have reached the required standards for QTS.

The QTS standards and the ITT requirements that apply to all ITT programmes in England are those imposed by the Secretary of State for Education under the Education (School Teacher's Qualifications) (England) Regulations 2003, which are made under sections 132, 145 and 210 of the Education Act 2002. The regulations set out the required standards that must be met by trainee teachers before they can be awarded QTS and the requirements for ITT providers for making recommendations for the award of QTS. There is a requirement for trainee teachers to meet all of the standards before they can be awarded QTS. These specific standards are those relevant to all professionals who are involved in ITT; this may include teacher training providers, qualified teachers and those who employ and support newly qualified teachers.

Diversity

The QTS standards related to the knowledge and understanding of achievement and diversity are listed under three different areas:

1. Q18 – trainee teachers are expected to understand how children and young people develop and that the progress and well-being of learners are affected by a range of developmental, social, religious, ethnic, cultural and linguistic influences. The TDA (2003) in its explanation of this quality states that teachers are able to recognize the influences that affect how young people learn, and that they must be able to understand how they develop and what learning and teaching can be improved for young people:

   > It is important for teachers to have a full and accurate understanding of the needs of each learner so that they can deploy a range of skills to tailor provision in ways that challenge, promote achievement and secure progress. Those who might be at risk depend on teachers and a range of other colleagues with specific responsibilities to monitor and manage their learning and well-being to provide them with the support they need. (Training and Development Agency, 2003, p. 1)

   The TDA (2003) states that these groups include those with special educational needs or disabilities, those from minority ethnic groups (including those for whom English is an additional language) and also those who may be from disadvantaged socioeconomic backgrounds and eligible for free school meals. It also mentions those children and young people who may be vulnerable owing to experiencing bullying (be it racist, homophobic or other forms of bullying).

2. Q19 – trainee teachers are expected to know how to make effective personalized provision for those whom they teach (including those for whom English is an additional language) or those who have specifically educational needs or disabilities. The standards state that trainee teachers should know how to 'take practical account of diversity and promote equality and inclusion in their teaching'. They also state that trainees should be able to account for the diversity of young people's learning through achieving personalized and individual learning by an inclusive approach to professional practice. They should do this by knowing '. . . how information gathered about standards and achievement across the school helps them to identify and plan for the learning needs of diverse groups and individuals, to ensure that they make the best possible progress' (Training

and Development Agency, 2003, p. 1). The standards also mention that trainee teachers should be aware of the duty placed on schools to promote community cohesion and should identify opportunities to contribute to this.

3. Q20 – trainee teachers are expected to know and understand the role of colleagues with specific responsibilities for learners with special educational needs and disabilities and other individual learning needs:

> Trainees need to know and understand the range of roles and responsibilities undertaken across the workforce in schools, and understand how the coordination of these roles can support learners. They need to know who is responsible for meeting the learning needs of specific groups. (Training and Development Agency, 2003, p. 1) (www. tda.gov.uk/trainee-teacher/qts-standards.aspx)

Other standards that trainee teachers are required to meet include *attributes* (relationships with young people, frameworks, communicating with others and personal professional development); *knowledge and understanding* (teaching and learning, assessment and monitoring, subjects and curriculum, literacy, numeracy and ICT, achievement and diversity [as discussed above], and health and well-being); *skills* (planning, teaching, assessing, monitoring and giving feedback, reviewing teaching and learning, learning environment, and team work and collaboration).

Community cohesion

The Education and Inspections Act (2006) introduced a duty to promote community cohesion in all maintained schools in England. The emphasis was on schools building positive relationships with all pupils, emphasizing a sense of shared values and encouraging pupils to feel part of a community at all levels (local, national and international). The guidance that exists on community cohesion explains some of the things that schools should be doing to promote such cohesion and how practices can be used in everyday teaching. Part of this is designed also to raise standards in schools with a focus on more (and more effective) engagement with local communities.

Community cohesion is defined as:

> . . . working towards a society in which there is a common vision and sense of belonging by all communities; a society in which the diversity of people's

backgrounds and circumstances is appreciated and valued; a society in which similar life opportunities are available to all; and a society in which strong and positive relationships exist and continue to be developed in the workforce, in schools and in the wider community. (HMSO, 2007, p. 3)

The term 'community' includes the school community, the community in which the school is located, the UK community and the global community. The guidance states that the school's contribution to community cohesion should be based on teaching, learning and the curriculum (helping pupils to understand others and diversity); equity and excellence (to ensure that equal opportunities enable all pupils to succeed); and engagement and extended services (to enable pupils to interact with those from different backgrounds to ensure greater tolerance).

The Equality Act 2010

The Equality Act 2010 came into force on 1 October 2010; it was part of the Labour Party's manifesto commitment to equality in the general election in 2005. The main aim of the Act was to simplify the law on discrimination by bringing together different types of legislation into one Act. The Equality Act replaced the Equal Pay Act (1970), the Sex Discrimination Act (1975), the Race Relations Act (1976), the Disability Discrimination Act (1995) and the Employment Equality Regulations (2003, 2006). The new Equality Act thereby facilitates a cross-cutting legislative framework that enhances the rights of individuals to advance equality of opportunity. Its aim is to simplify and to strengthen the previous legislation on equality and to deliver a more accessible framework of discrimination law that protects individuals from unequal and unfair treatment and so promote a more equal and just society. The goal of the Equality Act is to provide a major simplification of discrimination legislation that makes the law easier to understand and comply with, and to deliver significant benefits for individuals and public bodies.

All schools in the UK (irrespective of how they are funded) have obligations under the Equality Act and local authorities and education authorities have obligations under the schools provisions where they are responsible for the school body. What is new about the Act is that it introduces 'protected characteristics', which means that pupils are protected from discrimination and harassment based on 'protected characteristics'. These are disability, gender reassignment, pregnancy and maternity, race, religion or belief, sex and sexual orientation.

Unlawful discrimination in the Act is defined as direct discrimination, indirect discrimination, discrimination arising from disability and failures to make reasonable adjustments (for disabled people).

In terms of higher education in the UK, the public sector equality duties are equality legislation that gives public bodies (including further and HEIs) legal responsibilities to be able to demonstrate that they are taking action on equality in policy-making, the delivery of their services and public sector employment. The duties require public bodies to take steps to eliminate unlawful discrimination and harassment and actively to promote equality in their organizations. The duties provide a framework that will help institutions to tackle disadvantage – for example, the participation rates of White and minority ethnic students and gender stereotyping of subjects. Under the Equality Act, however, the single public sector equality duty requires public authorities to eliminate discrimination, harassment and victimization, advance equality of opportunity and foster good relations.

The Australian context

In Australia, teacher training (more generally known as pre-service teacher education) takes place in universities and other designated higher education providers. While most government funding to Australian universities is the responsibility of the Commonwealth Government, universities are mostly established by Acts of their respective State and Territory Governments. In keeping with this situation, university faculties or schools of teacher education have their teacher training programmes accredited by their respective State and Territory teacher registration authorities, such as the Queensland College of Teachers (www.qct.edu.au/). These authorities have exercised significant influence over the content and design of teacher training programmes, while allowing for considerable institutional autonomy and variation in programme implementation.

A recent and ongoing development has been the elaboration of an Australian national set of teacher professional standards, under the aegis of the Australian Institute of Teaching and School Leadership (www.aitsl.edu.au/). These standards were endorsed by Commonwealth, State and Territory Ministers for Education in December 2010, and are due to begin being implemented in 2013.

Australian national professional standards for teachers

There are currently seven national professional standards for teachers in Australia in the framework due to begin in 2013, clustered around three teaching domains:

Teaching domain 1: Professional knowledge

  Standard 1: Know students and how they learn
  Standard 2: Know the content and how to teach it

Teaching domain 2: Professional practice

  Standard 3: Plan for and implement effective teaching and learning
  Standard 4: Create and maintain supportive and safe learning environments
  Standard 5: Assess, provide feedback and report on student learning

Teaching domain 3: Professional engagement

  Standard 6: Engage in professional learning
  Standard 7: Engage professionally with colleagues, parents/carers and the
    community

On the assumption that teachers' capacities, and hence their demonstration of professional competence, develop over time, these seven standards are also associated with descriptors of four professional career stages: graduate, proficient, highly accomplished and lead (retrieved from www.teacherstandards.aitsl.edu. au/Standards/Overview).

References to issues of diversity and inclusion occur mostly in relation to the first standard, 'Know students and how they learn'. Specific examples of the character and tenor of these references are found in some of the career stage descriptors related to specific focus areas based on that standard. For example, the graduate stage descriptor for the focus area '1.1 Physical, social and intellectual development and characteristics of students' is 'Demonstrate knowledge and understanding of physical, social and intellectual development and characteristics of students and how these may affect learning' (retrieved from www.teacherstandards.aitsl.edu.au/Standards/AllStandards/1). Similarly, the proficient stage descriptor for the focus area '1.3 Students with diverse linguistic, cultural, religious and socioeconomic backgrounds' is 'Design and implement teaching strategies that are responsive to the learning strengths and needs of students from diverse linguistic, cultural, religious and socioeconomic backgrounds' (retrieved from www.teacherstandards.aitsl.edu.au/Standards/

AllStandards/1). Furthermore, the highly accomplished stage descriptor for the focus area '1.4 Strategies for teaching Aboriginal and Torres Strait Islander students' is 'Provide advice and support colleagues in the implementation of effective teaching strategies for Aboriginal and Torres Strait Islander students using knowledge of and support from community representatives' (retrieved from www.teacherstandards.aitsl.edu.au/Standards/AllStandards/1). And the lead stage descriptor for the focus area '1.6 Strategies to support full participation of students with disability' is 'Initiate and lead the review of school policies to support the engagement and full participation of students with disability and ensure compliance with legislative and/or system policies' (retrieved from www. teacherstandards.aitsl.edu.au/Standards/AllStandards/1).

Given that, as noted above, these national professional standards for Australian teachers have not yet been implemented, it is too early to tell whether they will be effective and how they will impact on Australian teacher training. Nevertheless, there is a considerable body of research already published (see for example Ingvarson, 2011) about the development of the standards and about wider issues of increased accountability and surveillance of teachers and teacher educators. For instance, Bourke, Ryan and Lidstone (2012/in press) propose that '. . . both students and . . . teachers themselves are better served when teachers assert their own definition of professionalism and thus reclaim their professional territory, rather than being compliant with generic governmental agendas'. Relatedly, Santor, Reid, Mayer and Singh (2012) pose the mind-concentrating question: '. . . will standards that are prescriptive and closely linked to accreditation requirements give us the flexibility to design teacher education curriculum that will help us prepare the next generation of teachers for a future that we don't yet understand?' (p. 1). By contrast, one Australian teacher educator cited by Kirby and Crawford (2012) states the case for these kinds of national professional teacher standards:

> . . . help[ing] to refocus . . . and to put some accountability into teacher education courses, [so] that we're not just a law unto ourselves – we just teach our units according to what we want but that there is a set of broader goals and outcomes out there that we need to make sure we're achieving. (p. 20)

Australian legislation related to diversity and inclusion

Like the UK and other Western countries, Australia has enacted a number of pieces of legislation designed to protect diversity and promote inclusion. For example, they are currently four principal national anti-discrimination laws in effect:

- The *Racial Discrimination Act 1975*
- The *Sex Discrimination Act 1984*
- The *Disability Discrimination Act 1992*
- The *Age Discrimination Act 2004.*

A fifth Act, the Australian Human Rights Commission Act 1986, '… establishes the Australian Human Rights Commission and regulates the processes for making and resolving complaints under the other four Acts' (Australian Commonwealth Attorney-General's Department, 2011, p. 5).

Also like the UK and other Western countries, the effectiveness of Australia's anti-discrimination legislation in protecting diversity and promoting inclusion has been debated widely in the scholarly literature (see for example Allen, 2010; Augoustinos & Every, 2010; O'Neill, 2011). According to Smith and Allen (2011), for instance, Australia has adopted '… an individual fault-based model of discrimination regulation … which targets only discrimination that can be traced to a wrong-doer' (p. 31), and furthermore:

> … Australia's anti-discrimination laws have not significantly developed since their inception, leaving Australia with ineffective laws and lagging behind international consensus on human rights and equality. To avoid achieving nothing more than 'consolidation' of narrow, inadequate, fault-based laws, we need to ask better questions. Addressing inequality is not just about fault. (p. 31)

Australia's legislation related to diversity and inclusion has similarly been critiqued from the perspective of its impact on, and in many cases its incapacity to assist, specific marginalized groups. These groups include Muslims (Bloul, 2008), people with disabilities (Poed & Keen, 2009), religious minorities (Parkinson, 2007) and women in the paid workforce (Baird, Williamson, & Heron, 2012). Sayed and Kramar (2009) provide a representative synthesis of the current situation: 'The legal framework in Australia places only limited obligations on organisations to manage cultural diversity. As a consequence, while a range of organisational responses have proliferated, an integrated approach towards managing culturally diverse workers is absent. … [U]nless cultural diversity is tackled at multiple levels and in a more integrated way, any attempt to either understand or manage such diversity may prove unrealistic' (p. 96).

To this point in the chapter, we have outlined key elements of the UK and Australian contexts pertaining to teacher training and national legislation related to diversity and inclusion. We argue that these elements reflect important theoretical understandings of identity that frame manifestations of 'race', gender and culture, and that impact significantly on educational policy and practice in both countries, in higher education as well as in other sectors. These theoretical understandings in turn evoke ongoing debates about the most appropriate and effective ways of engaging with them, such as by means of guidelines, laws and standards. It is precisely because those debates continue and elude finalization that trainee teachers and teacher educators must work hard to negotiate their journeys through veritable mazes of meaning- and decision-making and to find ways to protect diversity and promote inclusion within their respective spheres of activity and influence.

Empirical examples

In this section of the chapter, we present a number of empirical examples of these theoretical understandings of identity. In particular, we analyse how many of the participants in the first-named author's research linked their theoretical understandings of 'race' to specific issues of diversity and inclusion and how those broader concepts are played out in classrooms.

White and Black identities

For many of the respondents, the concept of identity was filtered through their experiences and understandings of their own identities. From that perspective, the notion of being White and being Black was related to visible markers of difference, and identity was seen as being marked out and sometimes unchanging and sometimes not. What is clear, though, is that the majority of respondents saw their own identity as White as being one of privilege, advantage and benefit in all situations. Many of the respondents remarked that they had often witnessed Black identity being viewed in negative and derogatory terms, with some respondents reporting that they had identified racism themselves. Racism at times was difficult for respondents to understand. On the one hand, respondents saw it as abhorrent and unacceptable. On the other hand, one respondent tried to justify racism in relation to personal experience and said that using racist words was not necessarily racist in the way that it would lead to violence (say, for example, as might be the case with the British National Party).

Teaching about 'race', diversity and inclusion

All of the respondents indicated that they did not feel that they had sufficient information about how to teach students about 'race', diversity and inclusion. The information that they had received in their courses was limited. Each time that issues of 'race', diversity and inclusion were discussed in lectures, they were usually approached as part of other inequalities (such as class and gender), rather than on their own as discrete subjects. Furthermore, the only courses that were available on these issues were optional Special Study courses that students could choose. The respondents were certainly not confident that they knew how to deal with issues of racism in the classroom, should they arise. All were sure, however, that they would not tolerate such behaviour and would immediately report it to their Head of Year and/or to their Head teacher.

What is clear from the above findings is strong endorsement of the proposition that trainee teachers require greater information and knowledge about issues to do with 'race', diversity and inclusion. In order to be effective teachers in the classroom, they must be able to understand how these terms are understood from a theoretical perspective and how these would be translated in the classroom. Here the curriculum itself has to be refocused to be more inclusive, by including the experiences of a diverse range of pupils to fit in with the needs of a multicultural society. The curriculum has to be reshaped and reworked to ensure that there is greater emphasis on inclusion as a thread that runs through the whole curriculum and its individual courses, rather than its being only a segment or an individual part of the curriculum. This should fit in with the whole ethos of the teacher training programme, which also includes thinking about the selection of courses and of the staff members who teach team in ways that reflect the diversity of the pupil population in schools.

From this perspective, we agree with Berlak and Moyenda (2001) that the main focus of critical multiculturalism 'is naming and actively challenging racism and other forms of injustice, not simply recognising and celebrating differences and reducing prejudice' (p. 92). Moreover, multicultural social justice education:

> ... starts with the premise that equity and justice should be goals for everyone and that solidarity across differences is needed to bring about justice. The notions of equity and justice point to not just a goal of equal opportunity

but also to one of equal results for diverse communities. (Sleeter & Grant, 2009, pp. 197–8)

Several strategies have been identified for the provision of a social justice agenda (Ladson-Billings, 1995). We contend that changing the curriculum for all trainee teachers would have a significant impact on how trainee teachers view issues to do with 'race', diversity and inclusion, and in turn social justice issues. But equally we also encourage a greater emphasis on the numbers of minority ethnic students recruited into teacher training programmes. We have a strong commitment to the ideal that teachers themselves can be 'agents of social change' (Darling-Hammond & Bransford, 2005). Social justice then can be promoted through the increased recruitment and retention of minority ethnic students enrolled in teacher training programmes. It has been argued that a more diverse teaching population is required to meet the needs of a diverse student intake (Villegas & Davis, 2008), and furthermore that a diverse staff body is needed to create learning conditions that are conducive to providing a social justice agenda (Sleeter, 2007).

One UK case-study university

One of the universities that participated in the research reported here and conducted by the first-named author was taking direct measures to respond to the demand to make the teaching workforce in the UK more diverse. This included providing opportunities for candidates with disabilities and candidates from BME groups that are currently under-represented in teaching. Currently the secondary PGCE course recruits approximately 6% of its candidates from BME backgrounds, whereas targets to increase the diversity of the workforce run at around 12%. There is a social necessity and a political will to rebalance staff representation in the education system where BME staff are currently heavily under-represented or employed in lowly paid positions.

In schools in the South East of England, for example, 11% of children from 5–18 are BME; however, BME teachers represent only 3% of the teaching staff. The TDA statistics gathered from ITT providers show a considerable under-representation of BME undergraduates and postgraduates in the region and recorded numbers show a current decline over previous years. The following data provide a more detailed analysis:

- BME recruitment across the South East is lower than the national target (currently 12%) and has decreased in 2008–9 compared with the two previous years.

- The South East is the third lowest of all Government Office Regions in both primary and secondary BME recruitment.
- Recruitment levels for 2008–9 are 4% for primary and 9% for secondary (compared with 9% and 14% respectively as the national averages).
- There is a considerable range across providers. For primary, the highest BME percentage recruited is 6% and the lowest is 0%. Secondary ranges from 2% to 13%.
- The TDA has provided annual grants to providers for BME recruitment/ retention activities.
- Despite this, a substantial number of providers find it consistently hard to meet their TDA BME advisory targets in spite of efforts to do so.
- Nationally the BME trainee retention rate on ITT programmes is about 50% lower than that for non-BME trainees.
- Some providers have noted differences in progress between BME and non-BME trainees. In 2006–7, 60 BME trainees in the region failed to attain QTS.
- Anecdotal evidence suggests that in some areas BME trainees find more difficulty in obtaining permanent posts. Only 66% of BME trainees registered employment in 2006–7, 15% fewer than non-BME trainees (Training and Development Agency, 2009).

The evidence points very clearly to the fact that many providers in the region have current and recurrent difficulties in improving the recruitment, retention and employment rates of BME teacher trainees in spite of the support that they receive. Our data corroborate this more general picture of trainee recruitment across the South East. However, once recruited their success rate varies. In 2008–9 the statistics of completion for BME showed 14 BME trainees recruited (5%); all candidates from Asian groups achieved success on the programme, although conversion to employment varied. Despite success, two of the Asian candidates have still not achieved employment, even though they have reported looking continuously. For Black British and Black African candidates (five on the course in 2008–9), only one of these candidates succeeded in gaining employment, although it is important to note that the lack of supported funding for overseas trainees in teacher training programmes does mean that retaining overseas trainees on these programmes can be difficult. Withdrawals owing to fee problems and/or other reasons were recorded reasons for the difficulties of achievement in this group. European nationals do well in the programme, including Polish and Finnish teachers. Attempts to create better opportunities for increasing diversity are contingent upon joint efforts with partnership schools to enable equal opportunity at the level of entry to ITE programmes, through the training and ultimately into employment.

Overall, ethnic minorities are under-represented at the majority of Russell Group universities (Race into Higher Education, 2010). Furthermore, as we have seen from our research, the employability chances of minority ethnic secondary PGCE students at this institution is poor, and minority ethnic graduates are failing to find jobs as easily as their White counterparts. A total of 66% of White students who graduated in 2007–8 found work within a year compared to just 56.3% of minority ethnic students (Race into Higher Education, 2010). With nearly half of the population of students studying education compared to White students, these are areas of concern that have to be addressed in developing strategies for success for those from minority ethnic backgrounds (5.8% of minority ethnic students compared to 10.3% of White students study education) (Race into Higher Education, 2010). This demonstrates that these issues of the inclusion of minority ethnic students in the areas that we highlight above are important not only for the recruitment and retention issues but also to address issues of the inclusion of these groups within the community and outreach work.

In one of the universities where we conducted our research, the programme has published its position on supporting BME trainees in publicity material and in the handbook alerting trainees to university-wide equal opportunity and race equality polices. In 2008–9 the reporting of a racist incident that targeted a trainee teacher was supported through the tutor system in partnership with the school. The pupils involved in racially harassing the trainee teacher were duly reprimanded through the host school's race equality policies. The incident was reported through the partnership in order to share good practice and to demonstrate the partners' commitment to anti-racism.

We also argue that students (of both White and Black backgrounds) should be encouraged to discuss openly their own experiences of racism and their respective perspectives as Black or White students. For some, this may be a difficult process, but it would encourage students to face these issues head on and examine what their positions mean in terms of teaching and aiming for a social justice agenda. Nieto (2010) argues that White students should think about their own White privileged identity, but set aside any guilt to think about how they can make positive changes for those who continue to remain marginalized and disadvantaged both in society and in education. There is also a need to examine and question the discourse of Whiteness and White identity (Leonardo, 2009).

Care has to be taken so that trainee teachers can build on these experiences, rather than simply leading towards reinforcing stereotypes (see Haberman & Post, 2008):

> To teach lessons about race and racism in teacher education is to struggle to unlearn racism itself – to interrogate the assumptions that are deeply embedded in the curriculum, to own our own complicity in maintaining existing systems of privilege and oppression, and to grapple with our own failure. (Cochran-Smith, 2000, p. 59)

The ultimate aim of these objectives is to try to tackle inequalities in education and to provide equal access to all students (regardless of their ethnic or class backgrounds) (see also Nieto, 2010). Within this objective, it is equally important for ITT providers to examine their own policies and attitudes of staff to explore whether the policies are in fact inclusive and how they work in practice. When addressing stereotypes, trainee teachers must question their own pedagogy and practice when thinking about how some minority ethnic students are failing at schools and in the education system, rather than placing blame on the families (Chubbick, 2010; Sleeter, 2008). Moreover, 'Ethics and the distribution of power, status and rewards are basic societal concerns; education *must* address them' (original emphasis) (Nieto, 2010, p. 77; *italics in original*).

This chapter has examined selected theoretical understandings of identity, particularly focused on 'race', diversity and inclusion, in the UK and Australia. Those understandings were analysed by means of their enactments in teacher training policies and standards, national legislation and empirical data from a recent research project. This continuing and recursive interplay between the conceptual and the practical, between the ideal and the material, is crucial to the approach taken in this book to deconstructing and demystifying identity and its intersection with pedagogy. That is, individual trainee teachers' and teacher educators' constructions and experiences of identity derive from, and are framed by, powerful and profound theoretical ideas. At the same time, those ideas take form and exert influence only in the particular contexts of specific groups and communities. Central among those contexts is higher education.

Identity and the Context of Higher Education

This chapter explores the workings of higher education in the UK and Australia. It outlines the different higher education systems in the UK and Australia and explores inequalities of 'race', class and gender and how these inequalities impact on the academy and student experiences. The chapter analyses the workings of both higher education systems and examines these within their different social contexts, as a prelude to interrogating their respective approaches to teacher training that are outlined in the following chapter.

The UK context

Different types of universities

In Great Britain universities are founded by Acts of Parliament and, in order for universities (or other institutions) to be granted status to award degrees to students, they must be recognized by the Privy Council, which is an advisory body to the government and the state, and which is the mechanism in the British state through which agreement is reached by Privy Councillors rather than government ministers. Most British universities are funded but not owned by the state, compared to other countries such as the USA where many universities are both publicly and privately funded.

There are four main types of universities in Britain:

1. Ancient universities – these were founded before the nineteenth century and are seen to be the most prestigious of the British universities. These include the Universities of Oxford, Cambridge, Edinburgh, Glasgow, St Andrews, Aberdeen and Dublin. Oxford and Cambridge are the top two and most

prestigious universities in Britain and frequently score very highly in league tables. Together they are known as 'Oxbridge'.

2. Red Brick universities – these were set up in the Victorian era and offered practical subjects such as engineering (but also academic subjects) to students. Examples of Red Brick universities include the Universities of Birmingham, Southampton, Newcastle, Manchester and Bristol.

3. Plate Glass universities – owing to their modern architectural appearance, these universities became known as Plate Glass universities and were set up in the 1960s after the *Robbins Report*. Examples of these universities include the Universities of Sussex, Warwick, Lancaster, York, Kent and Brunel.

4. 'New' universities – these are former polytechnics that were given university status post-1992 during the Conservative government under John Major. Many tend not to have high reputations compared to the above three tiers and appear quite low in league tables. Examples of post-1992 universities include the Universities of East London, Greenwich, Hertfordshire, Derby and Coventry.

University groupings

Many of the universities described above have formed their own groups based on their research, teaching and ethos. These groups are based on universities that share similar ideas, procedures and strategies for improving their quality in research and teaching. These groups are split into five types:

1. The Russell Group, which represents 24 universities, and which is:

> . . . committed to maintaining the very best research, an outstanding teaching and learning experience and unrivalled links with business and the public sector. The members of the Russell Group have the quality and strengths to compete successfully in the global market place for research, skills, expertise and funding. (www.russellgroup.ac.uk/about-russell-group)

Members of the Russell Group include the Universities of Oxford, Cambridge, Bristol, Southampton, Birmingham, Manchester, Warwick, Edinburgh and Glasgow.

2. The 1994 Group of universities, which:

> . . . represents 19 of the UK's most research-intensive and internationally renowned universities. The 1994 Group's mission is to promote excellence

in research and teaching. Seeking to promote excellence in the student experience is therefore at the very heart of what we do. Each member institution delivers an extremely high standard of education to its students, demonstrating excellence in teaching and academic support, and providing learning in a research-rich community. (www.1994group. ac.uk/aimsandvalues)

Members of the 1994 Group include the Universities of Surrey, Sussex and York as well as Goldsmiths College, London and the Institute of Education, London.

3. The Million+ Group of universities, which describe themselves as 'a university think-tank' that uses:

> . . . rigorous research and evidence-based policy to solve complex problems in higher education. We publish research reports and policy papers and we submit evidence to parliamentarians, government and other agencies. Our member institutions pride themselves on diversity, flexibility and opportunity, each has its own specialities, qualities and principles, but together they provide a network of institutions that truly promote aspiration, excellence and innovation. (www.millionplus.ac.uk/ who/index)

Members of the Million+ Group include the Universities of East London, Kingston, Buckinghamshire, Wolverhampton and South Bank.

4. The University Alliance Group, which comprises 23 business focused universities formed in 2006 and which consists of both pre- and post-1992 new universities:

> The member institutions have a balanced portfolio of research, teaching, enterprise and innovation integral to their missions and represent a strong voice from the middle sector making a vital contribution to the prosperity of the country. (www.university-alliance.ac.uk/about-the-alliance.htm)

Their strength lies in their close links with industry and economy. Members of the University Alliance Group include the Universities of Portsmouth, Plymouth, Lincoln, Hertfordshire and Huddersfield.

5. The UKADIA (the United Kingdom Arts and Design Institutions Association) is a group of specialist art and design institutions that consist of different higher and further education institutions. Their focus is:

> . . . to promote, nationally and internationally, the key contributions of specialist colleges to the UK's world-renowned reputation in visual arts,

performance and the creative and cultural industries and to work together as a network to widen participation in Higher Education to encourage mobility into professions serving the creative and cultural industries. (www.ukadia.ac.uk/)

Their members include the Royal College of Art, the Ravensbourne College of Art, the University for the Creative Arts, University College Falmouth and the Plymouth College of Art.

Higher and further education in the UK

In order to understand the current situation with higher education in the UK, it is necessary to explain how it has been affected by further education. Further education colleges in England were nationalized under the Conservative government in 1993; this meant that they were no longer under the control of the local education authorities. Consequently the colleges were given status as charities and were able to operate under their own control (making their own strategic decisions on employment, pay and conditions) rather than remaining under the direct control of the government (Ainley & Allen, 2010).

Owing to recent changes in funding, further education colleges may well return to receiving their funding directly from their respective local authorities (under the new Coalition Government elected in 2010). It has been argued that many students who enter further education do so because of their failures in the schooling system, and as a result the pressure on the further education system is vast as it tries to address students' needs by offering them a variety of vocational and technical skills (Ainley & Allen, 2010).

In 2004, the Labour Government launched their pre-budget report (*Skills in the Global Economy*), which outlined the low proportion of young people who remained in education after the age of 16. The report was launched as there were concerns that those who left school at the age of 16 had limited levels of formal education and lacked skills that they could use in the labour market. This report raised important concerns about the levels of literacy and numeracy of young people in the UK and as a result the Labour Government commissioned the *Leitch Report*, which examined concerns that the UK was lagging behind other European and international countries and was unable to compete in the now globalized labour market. This was due to poor levels of literacy and numeracy in the labour market as well as the UK's ranking in the Organization for Economic Co-operation and Development (OECD).

The 2006 *Leitch Review* found that, despite the increasing numbers of graduates, there was still little that provided young people with skills that equipped them to deal with the demands of the labour market. The *Leitch Review* recommended that by 2020 the UK should aim to be a world leader in the provision of skills for the labour market and to rank highly in OECD tables (compared to 12th out of 18, which was the position previous to the publication of the report). The report concluded that by 2020:

1. 95% of adults should have the basic skills of numeracy and literacy;
2. 90% of adults should be qualified to level 2 (5 GCSEs or equivalent);
3. there should be a balance of intermediate skills with an increase in those having 2 or more A levels (level 3); and
4. more than 40% of adults should be qualified to level 4 and above (equivalent to degree level).

The *Leitch Review* also emphasized the importance of shared responsibility among individuals, employers and the government whereby there should be greater investment in education and training so that employers could contribute to the training and skills provided to employees. The emphasis on the provision of vocational education and training would mean that employers could be directly involved in the types and provision of training that they offered to their employees. Following recommendations from the *Leitch Review*, the Labour Government set up the *UK Commission for Employment and Skills* (which superseded the *Sector Skills Development Agency* and the *National Employment Panel*). The main responsibilities of the UK Commission were: to assess the progress of the UK towards its aim of becoming a world class leader in employment and skills by 2020 (as recommended by the *Leitch Review*); to advise government on labour market skills policy-making; to monitor the UK's labour market skills systems; to promote greater investment in developing the workforce; and to manage the *Sector Skills Council*.

Following the publication of the *Leitch Review*, there have been significant changes in the strategic approaches concerning the training of young people and adults. This has included an increase in the numbers of government-funded training opportunities available for those aged 14–19 as well as the range of entitlements available for this age group. The main reason for this change is so that young people can have access to different training opportunities through a variety of education providers in order to access greater choice in the subjects available to them. Part of this agenda has included the introduction of diplomas, the International Baccalaureate (taken from the European education model) and apprenticeships. To increase further the level of skills, the government has introduced the possibility of raising the statutory age at which young people can leave full-time education to 18 and consequently encouraging greater collaboration among a diversity of educational institutions. This means that young people will continue in education or training until their 17th birthday from 2013 and until age 18 from 2015. This will be the first time in 40 years that the school leaving has been raised in England.

However, as much of the public funding will be directed towards those achieving level 2 skills (5 GCSEs or equivalent), those wanting to improve their skills at levels 3 or 4 will experience greater financial difficulty and will be disadvantaged. Furthermore, the emphasis on increasing the number of those achieving level 4 qualifications (degree level) has actually contributed to a significant decline in the quality and value of degrees achieved in higher education, with significant numbers of students obtaining degrees with little or no worth (Ainley & Allen, 2010; Bhopal, 2010). Furthermore, the increase in student fees will create further barriers between 'old' and 'new' universities and lead to an even more divisive higher education system.

Widening participation?

The *Widening Participation Agenda* in higher education was a government education policy introduced under the New Labour Government in 2003 (*The Future of Higher Education*, DfES). Its main aim was to increase the numbers of young people entering higher education, particularly those from under-represented groups (and those disadvantaged groups who are less likely than others to enter higher education). The main aim of the Widening Participation Agenda was to increase participation in higher education to as much as 50% by 2010 and to readdress the balance of inequalities in participation in higher education between different social classes. This included young people from lower income families, those with disabilities and those from minority ethnic backgrounds.

However, despite the focus of the *Widening Participation Agenda*, inequalities in higher education persist. Recent research has shown that students from lower socioeconomic backgrounds and state schools are less likely to go to Oxbridge or Russell Group universities than those from middle-class backgrounds and those attending private schools (Higher Education Statistics Agency, 2008). The Sutton Trust (2004) argues that state school students are less likely to attend the more prestigious, 'red brick' universities than those from higher social class backgrounds (see also Watts, 2012). Furthermore, research has shown that students from minority ethnic and working-class backgrounds are more likely to study humanities subjects (such as the social sciences) and attend 'new' (post-1992) universities (as are working-class students) (Bhopal, 2010; Tolley & Rundele, 2006).

More recent research by the Higher Education Funding Council of England (HEFCE)[1] (2010) has shown that the gap among the social classes, and between the rich and the poor, is narrowing in relation to attending university, but the picture remains complex. The report argues that educationalists and the government must do more to increase the numbers of young people from poor and lower-class backgrounds attending prestigious universities (see also Watts, 2012). Universities themselves have put in place measures that help to widen access and participation for those from less privileged backgrounds; one way to do this is to set targets for the numbers of students whom they admit from such backgrounds. The report states that the admissions systems and processes are themselves fair but that:

> The evidence suggests that once candidates with the requisite talent and attainment are in the relevant applications pool, they are treated fairly and that, once they are admitted to university, similarly qualified students from less favoured backgrounds do at least as well as their peers. (2010, p. 8)

The report concludes that there has been a sustained increase in the rates of young people attending universities from poor and disadvantaged backgrounds since the mid-2000s and that widening participation policies in the last decade have therefore been successful.

HEFCE has introduced several measures and initiatives to encourage students from disadvantaged backgrounds to enter higher education such as financial initiatives as well as the *Aimhigher* programme. The *Aimhigher* programme works across schools and the further and higher education sector, specifically with the *Department for Business, Innovation and Skills* and the *Learning and Skills Council*. One example includes the *Aimhigher Associates Scheme*, which provides support and training for pupils in state schools for their transition into higher and further education.

Who goes to university?

Recent statistics released by the Higher Education Statistics Agency in England (Higher Education Statistics Agency 2011, SFR 153 Higher Education student enrolments and qualifications obtained at HEIs in the UK for the academic year 2009/10) show some changes in the pattern of participation in higher education. In terms of the total number of enrolments, there has been an increase of 4% from 2008/9. There has also been a 6% increase in full-time enrolments since 2008/9, with 44% of full-time enrolments in 2009/10 being in science subjects (which show no change from the previous year).

The number of first degree graduates has shown an increase of 5% from 2009/10. Of those gaining a first degree in 2009/10, 14% obtained a first class honours degree, the same as in 2009/10, and 48% obtained an upper second class degree, which was also the same as in 2009/10. A total of 57% of first degree graduates in 2009/10 were women, which was the same as in 2008/9. In 2009/10, 41% of first degree graduates achieved their degree in a Science subject, which was the same as in 2008/9. Of these graduates, 50% were women, which was the same as in 2008/9.

In terms of qualifications obtained, in 2009/10, the figures show an increase of 6% compared to 2008/9. There was an increase of 12% of students who obtained a postgraduate qualification in 2009/10.

There has also been change in the patterns of minority ethnic students' participation in British higher education. Recent research on the experiences of BME students in higher education shows a significant change from previous years. Research carried out by *Communities and Local Government* (Race into Higher Education, 2010) shows that the numbers of minority ethnic students (Black and Asian) in higher education has doubled from 8.3% in 1995–6 to 16% in 2007–8. This finding also shows that the proportion of minority ethnic students attending university is more than the total numbers in the UK population (which is 14.2%). The research also found that, within the category of 'minority ethnic', it is the British Indian group that is the best represented in UK universities, but the Black group and Black British Africans have tripled their university presence in the last 12 years.

However, the picture of disadvantage still remains, with BME students continuing to be under-represented at Oxbridge and Russell Group universities. Their attendance is also polarized across UK universities depending on locality and the subjects that they choose to study. Students from minority ethnic backgrounds are more likely to attend universities in cities, namely London, or in areas where there are large numbers of minority ethnic populations. This has also been supported by empirical research that shows, for example, that British Asian women and African-Caribbean women are more likely to attend their local university where there is a 'critical mass' of students from similar backgrounds to themselves (see Bhopal, 2010; Bhopal & Takhar, 2010). The *Race into Higher Education Report* (2010) found that eight out of the ten universities with the highest proportion of minority ethnic students were in London and the Home Counties; the others were in Birmingham and Bradford, where there are high numbers of BME groups in the population.

The picture that emerges for subject choice is also interesting; for example, those from BME backgrounds are half as likely as other students to study education. Almost twice as many White students opt for education compared to those from minority ethnic backgrounds (the figures show that 10.3% of students who study education are from White backgrounds, compared with 5.8% from BME backgrounds). It has been argued that we need greater numbers of students from BME backgrounds to enter education to provide positive role models for children and young people (see Bhopal, Harris, & Rhamie, 2009; Davies & Crozier, 2008). However, for women from BME backgrounds, education is seen as the fifth most popular subject to study. The figures have risen from 5.3% of BME students choosing education in 1995–6 to 7.7% in 2007–8; however, the figure for White females remains at 13.3% (Race into Higher Education, 2010).

Male students from BME backgrounds, however, are more likely to study business and administration courses compared to their White peers. There are increasing numbers of women from BME backgrounds opting for medicine; these figures have shown a significant increase from 12 years ago. For those students from Asian backgrounds, law is one of the most popular subjects for those from British Pakistani and British Bangladeshi backgrounds. However, the most popular subjects for British Indians are medicine and dentistry.

The impact of tuition fees on higher education

The *Dearing Report* (The National Committee of Inquiry into Higher Education, 1997) was a major study that examined the future of higher education in the UK in 1997. It was commissioned by the Labour Government and its aims were to provide a comprehensive review of the state of higher education since the *Robbins Report*, which was published in the 1960s (Report of the Committee on Higher Education, 1963). The report made a significant number of recommendations about higher education, but the most important recommendation was a change from funding undergraduates by government grants to a system in which tuition fees supported by a low interest government loan were introduced.

Following the *Dearing Report*, in October 2010, the *Browne Review* (An Independent Review of Higher Education Funding and Student Finance, 2010) was published and its main aim was to consider the future of higher education funding in England. Its main recommendation was to remove the cap on fees so that universities could charge their own amounts, which would mean that graduates would pay back their student loans when they earned around £21,000. The government would provide loans to cover tuition fees and living costs for some students, but means-tested grants would be available for students from lower income backgrounds. Part-time students would not have to pay tuition fees. The review did not recommend a graduate tax as it would not provide enough funding to foot the bill for the cost of higher education.

The *Browne Review* (An Independent Review of Higher Education Funding and Student Finance, 2010) contends that introducing tuition fees (without a cap in which universities could set their own fees) would in fact encourage universities to increase their standards and the quality of their teaching and research. This has been supported by the Director of the Russell Group Universities, Dr Wendy Piatt (Director-General of the Russell Group), who stated, 'By removing the cap in England, the expert team led by Lord Browne has rightly recognized that a substantial increase in graduate contributions is the only viable and the fairest way to secure this vital investment' (Russell Group response to the Browne Review of University Funding, 10 October 2010). Yet the Russell Group has been criticized for its lack of intake of students from working class and minority ethnic backgrounds. A recent report found that the representation of BME students in Russell Group Universities is unbalanced, with the four London-based universities having a high proportion, but the presentation outside London the representation being limited (see Race into Higher Education, 2010). Critics argue that such drastic measures to changes in higher education funding would in fact further prevent those from disadvantaged and lower income backgrounds from attending university, resulting in a more divisive and unequal higher education system, which would lead to further inequalities in the labour market and society more generally (see Bhopal & Preston, 2011).

In November 2010, the new Coalition Government introduced a cap on fees of £9000, with greater emphasis and pressure on universities to increase their widening participation agenda. It is proposed that the fees will be introduced in the 2012/13 academic year. The publication of the *Browne Review* (An Independent Review of Higher Education Funding and Student Finance, 2010) led to huge student protests in London and throughout the UK. At the time of writing, it is too early to predict the real impact of the Browne Review on higher education in the UK, but previous research has shown that an increase in student fees will further marginalize those from disadvantaged groups from attending universities, as well as influencing the types of courses that individuals choose and the degree of choice that they will have in attending particular universities (University of Leicester, 2010 (www2.le.ac.uk/ebulletin/news/press-releases/2010–2019/2010/09/nparticle.2010–09–20.5884706788).

With such significant changes occurring in higher education, research has questioned the value of obtaining a degree, particularly in the current social and economic climate (Ainley & Allen, 2010). In times of recession, the competition for jobs increases, with young people questioning the value of a degree (particularly if they feel that they will be laden with huge debts). Studies have shown that there are more graduates unemployed in the current economic recession than ever before; unemployment for graduates is now at the highest level for 17 years. A recent report by the Higher Education Careers Service Unit (What do graduates do, 2010) showed that only 57% of graduates found employment after graduating in the UK and that the number of graduates who were unemployed six months after graduating increased by 1% in 2009, increasing it to 8.9%. At the same time, given the increase in tuition fees due to be introduced in 2012–13, the numbers of young people opting for higher education continue to increase.

But if getting a degree does not increase the chances of better employment, what does it do? It certainly has little effect on social mobility, given that those from middle-class backgrounds continue to get middle-class jobs. If those from BME working-class backgrounds are disadvantaged in higher education, what chance do they have to succeed in the labour market? As Roberts argues, '. . . graduates discover their qualifications do not guarantee middleclass jobs – merely admission to the pools that are allowed to compete for these jobs' (Roberts, 2009, p. 162).

Consequently, the numbers of students who have no choice but to rely on part-time work to see them through university is on the increase. Furthermore, many of these students have no choice but to remain in the parental home in order to pay for the costs associated with attending university (Ainley & Allen, 2010; Bhopal, 2010). Ainley and Allen argue that such changes can have dire consequences for young people, who simply are no longer able to 'grow up' and become independent: '. . . declining employment opportunities, the increased burden of student debt for those who continue to higher education and also, as in Eastern Europe, the persistently unfavourable conditions in the housing market, effectively delay the process of transition still further' (2009, p. 104). The authors (Ainley & Allen, 2009) argue that even though, nearly half of young people enter higher education, there is only a small number of these who are able to go to the most prestigious and well-respected universities and even fewer are able to secure 'graduate jobs' (see also Williams & Filippakou, 2009). Contrary to this are those defined as the 'underclass' who have little or no chance of either entering education or finding secure employment.

Indeed, the numbers of young people unemployed will continue to rise, as will those classified as being 'NEETs' (Not in Education, Employment or Training – please see the next subsection in this chapter), given the recent cuts in funding at local and national levels. The government has introduced a 12% cut in central local government funding (see BBC News 12 December 2010, Core Funding cut by 12%). These cuts will affect not only the education budget but also all core services, which will affect all members of society. In Tony Blair's famous 'Education, Education, Education' speech in 2007, he argued that his target was for 50% of young people to attend universities and obtain a degree. It is possible that this target may have been achieved, but what has it meant for those young people who remain in debt, without a job and unable to buy their own property? It seems that young people have to continue to negotiate themselves through a 'risk society' (Beck, 1992; see also Furlong & Kelly, 2005; Threadgold & Nilan, 2009), which leads to greater uncertainty in fractured times.

NEETS

Young people not in education, employment or training are classified as NEETS in the UK. Recent statistical data released by the Department of Education in England (August 2010 statistics release) have shown that the number of 16–18-year-olds who are classed as being NEETs has shown a small increase from 195,000 in the first quarter of 2010 to 198,000 to the end of June in that year, although this is a marked decrease on the figures from the same time as last year. Figures given for those aged 19–24 have dropped from 733,000 to 677,000. There are variations on the figures depending on the ages of young people. For 16-year-olds, the numbers show the lowest level for a period of five years, but this may be due to the increase in the numbers of young people entering higher education. For 17-year-olds, the figure has shown some fluctuation, but a marked drop since 2009 is evident. For 18-year-olds, the figure is higher than five year ago and is three times the figure for 16-year-olds. This is explained by the falling numbers in employment (see also National Youth Agency).

The business of higher education?

With such significant changes occurring to higher education as those discussed above, recent research has argued that higher education has become a globalized industry, with an increase in the numbers of students from the European Union and elsewhere coming to the UK to study for their degrees (Ball, 2008). For example, in 2001 the OECD stated that the global student market was worth up to 350 billion US dollars. Ball (2008, p. 29) argues that in 2003–4 the international UK student industry was worth around 28 billion pounds, which was higher than the worth of the financial industry.

The globalization and marketization of higher education in the UK are compounded by the former Research Assessment Exercise (RAE) and the forthcoming Research Excellence Framework (REF) in which universities compete with one another for places in university league tables. Each university's position is measured by their degree of excellence in research and teaching. The exercise takes place every four years and the results are used to assess the amount of funding that each HEI receives from HEFCE. The RAE is also used as a measure by staff and postgraduate students (particularly PhD students) to assess excellence and quality in teaching. The next REF will take place in 2014. HEFCE states that the REF will 'inform the selective allocation of research funding to HEIs, provide benchmarking information and establish reputational yardsticks and provide accountability for public investment in research and demonstrate its benefits'. HEFCE also states that through the REF UK funding bodies will develop a dynamic and competitive research sector in which HEIs can compete for funding (www. hefce.ac.uk/research/ref/). Each HEI will be judged on three aspects: the quality of research outputs; the wider impact of the research; and the vitality of the research environment. Given the recent squeeze on HEI funding (October 2010 Coalition Government's Comprehensive Spending Review and 2011 Browne Review), it is anticipated that competition for external research funding from research councils will increase, which will have an impact on how HEIs are judged in the REF.

Given the financial investment in, and the impact of globalization on, higher education, students are now seen as consumers and customers in higher education. A degree has become a commodity that can be exchanged for a job in the labour market (if you're lucky!) (Ainley & Allen, 2009; Willmott, 1995). However, given the current number of graduates who remain unemployed, a degree does not even guarantee a job in the current economic and social climate and is unlikely to do so in the near future. As Ball argues:

> . . . as universities compete to maximize their income by seeking new 'markets' and reorienting themselves to the student customer, new forms of 'delivery' and consumption of HE are being created that can result in learning becoming increasingly fragmented and combined in novel ways with no guarantee of internal coherence. (2008, p. 23)

Consequently, we are moving towards a process of ongoing marketization and globalization in higher education in the UK.

The Australian context

Many of these features of the contemporary UK higher education context – including the increased marketization and globalization – are also evident in Australia, although they are sometimes manifested differently. Those differences reflect varied histories and current developments, as well as diverse enactments of the connections between higher education policy-making and provision and the constructions of individuals' and groups' identities – including in relation to inequalities of 'race', class and gender and how these inequalities are experienced by university students in both countries.

Different types of universities

Currently Australia has 39 universities (Universities Australia, 2012) established by Act of Parliament, whether at the Commonwealth or at the respective State or Territory Government level. Thirty-seven of them are publicly funded, and the other two are private, one established by an Australian businessman and the other by the Catholic Church. As in the UK, Australian universities vary widely in terms of longevity, focus and reputation, although they must all demonstrate conformity to certain Australian government requirements. Moreover, they are required to submit to regular audits of their quality related to teaching and learning (initially by the Australian Universities Quality Agency and now by the newly established Tertiary Education Quality and Standards Agency) and to research (initially by the Research Quality Framework and now by the Excellence in Research in Australia initiative by the Commonwealth Government).

Also as in the UK, Australian universities have undergone significant change in different periods with the development of Australian higher education. Previously a 'binary system' operated, whereby higher education providers were divided into universities and colleges of advanced education, the former awarding degrees at all levels, including doctorates, and the latter offering diplomas and bachelor degrees. John Dawkins, as Australian Minister for Employment, Education and Training between 1987 and 1991 in the Hawke Labor Government, oversaw the abolition of the binary system and the (in some cases forced) amalgamation of higher education providers into a larger number of universities. Dawkins also reintroduced university student fees (which had been abolished by the previous Labor Government of Gough Whitlam in 1973) in the form of the Higher Education Contribution Scheme (HECS) (Gale & Tranter, 2011).

Also as in the UK, Australian universities have been assigned to different types; sometimes these classifications are self-assigned, and sometimes they are assigned by other universities for purposes of competitive differentiation. One such typology was provided by Marginson and Considine (2000):

- The *Sandstone* universities, the oldest foundations in each state, including the universities of Sydney, Queensland, Adelaide and Western Australia. . . . All have some sandstone buildings. . . .
- The *Redbricks*, the strongest of the post-second world war universities, including the University of N[ew] S[outh] W[ales] and Monash University. Their political economy – size, academic role, incomes – is near interchangeable with that of the Sandstones. They had had less time to accumulate status benefits. Redbrick is more than evident in their architecture.
- The *Gumtrees*, universities founded later in the post-war period, between 1960 and 1975, the main period of publicly financed expansion. They include the Universities of Newcastle and Griffith, and James Cook, Deakin and Flinders Universities. Many of the sites were planted with native [tree]s (hence 'Gumtrees', though 'Acacias' or 'Banksias' are other possibilities) in contrast with the English gardens of the colonial period.
- The *Unitechs*, largest of the old C[olleges of] A[dvanced] E[ducation]s in five states, with a strong vocational and industry-orientation, including Queensland University of Technology and the University of Technology, Sydney. The architecture in this group is characteristically ugly, ranging from a grimy early Fordism/Taylorism, to utilitarian modern.

- The *New Universities*, a heterogeneous group of post-1986 foundations including Central Queensland, Southern Cross and Edith Cowan universities. In their buildings, utilitarian recency combines with secondary school leftovers from the CAE period. (p. 189; *italics in original*)

This typology shares some features to that outlined above for the four university types in the UK. For instance, some of the category descriptors in both countries evoke readily identifiable architectural and physical features, such as 'red brick' and 'plate glass' in the UK and 'sandstone' and 'gumtree' in Australia. More significantly, in both countries the descriptors highlight enduring disparities in status and in cultural and financial capital that in important respects parallel equally enduring disparities on the part of varied student groups in accessing higher education and then using that access as a springboard for empowering and transforming life chances.

University groupings

As in the UK, Australian universities have joined particular groupings with other institutions with similar features, partly for the protection and security afforded by being part of a larger set of organizations in what is an increasingly competitive and in many ways hostile environment. These groupings have been identified as follows:

- Group of Eight: like the Russell Group universities in the UK, 'the oldest universities in their mainland capital cities with the biggest research budgets and the biggest accumulations of academic, cultural and socio-economic capital' (Moodie, 2012a).
- Australian Technology Network: 'institutions that were established early as technical institutes in a capital city and formally designated a university after 1987' (Moodie, 2012a).
- Innovative Research Universities; this was formed by the 'gumtrees' universities and 'identifies with the UK's 1994 group' of universities (Moodie, 2012a).
- Regional Universities Network: 'in 2011 six universities which have their headquarters in a regional centre recently formed the Regional Universities Network'; 'universities with most of their student load in centres with a population of less than 250,000 people' (Moodie, 2012a).

According to the Australian Education Network (2012):

> These [university groupings] have been formed to promote the mutual objectives of the member universities. There are a number of objectives in this including marketing advantages, practical benefits of collaboration and the increased lobbying power that comes from being part of a group.

Higher and further education in Australia

As in the UK, Australian higher education is integrally connected with further education (also known as vocational education and training). For example, a number of Australian universities are 'dual sector', incorporating both higher and further education offerings and seeking to capitalize on the presumably heightened convergence afforded by combining both types of qualifications in a single institution. This convergence is evident also in the development of the Australian Qualifications Framework (2012), which provides a national listing of school and post-school qualifications and identifies pathways that students can take moving from one qualification to another.

These connections and this convergence take place despite some important structural and other differences between Australian higher and further education. For instance, while the Commonwealth Government funds universities, technical and further education institutes and colleges are funded by state and territory governments. Moreover, vocational education and training is also offered by private providers if they receive accreditation as registered training organizations. The field is thus highly differentiated and complex.

Part of that complexity is evident in significant variation on the extent to which post-school students are taking up the opportunity of the pathway between further and higher education, with largest numbers taking this pathway evident in nursing, education and information technology, and fewest opportunities in the natural and physical sciences and engineering and related technologies (Moodie, 2012b). Furthermore, nursing and education 'provide more opportunities for students from a low socioeconomic status background' (p. 143). Similarly, while the credit transfer arrangement for helping early childhood education students to move from vocational to university education 'was found to be satisfactory', 'gaps were identified' in the 'curriculum structures, teaching styles and assessment' (Whitington, Ebbeck, Diamond, & Yim, 2009, p. 27) in the two systems.

Widening participation?

Like the UK, Australia has a widening participation agenda for its university sector, although it is known by a number of other names, including student equity (Sellar & Gale, 2011) and social inclusion (Wood & Willems, 2012). Also like the UK, that agenda has had varied success. On the one hand:

> Over the last one hundred years, not only has Australian higher education participation significantly increased, but it now consists of a more diverse student population. . . . Women, once a minority among the privileged, now form the majority of students, although their enrolments are not evenly spread through course and award offerings. Other increases involve higher education participation rates of mature-age students, international students and students with disabilities . . . (Putman & Gill, 2011, p. 177)

On the other hand:

> . . . despite these developments, the higher education sector still remains inequitable in terms of socioeconomic background. Research consistently shows significantly lower proportions of low SES students attend university as compared with their higher SES peers . . . (Putman & Gill, 2011, p. 177)

More broadly, in 1990 the then Australian Commonwealth Department of Employment, Education and Training (1990) identified six disadvantaged groups whose access to higher education was less extensive and sustained than that of other groups in the Australian population: people from low socioeconomic backgrounds; Indigenous Australians; women in non-traditional areas; people from non-English-speaking backgrounds; people with disabilities; and people from rural and isolated areas (see also Putman & Gill, 2011). 'Recent years have seen significant improvements in tertiary access for women in non-traditional areas, people from non-English speaking backgrounds, and people with a disability . . .' (Putman & Gill, 2011, p. 177), and, as noted above, many Australian universities have their main campuses in non-metropolitan areas of the country, thereby seeking to cater directly for students living in regional and rural areas.

Despite these improvements, the *Bradley Report* (Bradley, Noonan, Nugent, & Scales, 2008), the latest in a long line of reviews of Australian higher education, contended that three of these six identified groups remained under-represented in terms of access to Australian higher education: '. . . Indigenous people, people with low socio-economic status, and those from regional and remote areas' (p. xi). The report recommended a number of ameliorating actions and associated targets by the year 2020, including increasing the proportion of Australians aged between 25 and 34 attaining at least a bachelor degree from 29% to 40%, and raising the proportion of enrolled undergraduates from low socioeconomic backgrounds from 15% to 20%.

Certainly Putman and Gill (2011) concurred that '. . . the low SES group was proving a more intransigent problem than the other groups' (p. 177) (see also Devlin & O'Shea, 2012/in press). However, they argued that a significant dimension of the problem derives from the complexity of defining 'socioeconomic status', as well as from doubts about '. . . the degree to which current universities are prepared to take more non-traditional students' (p. 181). They elaborated four strategies that they asserted that universities can implement in order to attract and retain low socioeconomic status students:

- 'Outreach support through the schools' (p. 183)
- 'Financial support' (p. 183)
- 'Cultural change' (p. 184)
- 'Academics: Re-education and curriculum change' (p. 186).

By implication, the current manifestations of all four of these foci function as barriers to low socioeconomic status students participating in Australian higher education. Also by implication, all four of these proposed strategies should be targeted as well as other under-represented groups, including Indigenous Australians, and rural and isolated residents. Certainly Putman and Gill (2011) have no doubt about '. . . the need for significant change in the culture and practices of Australian universities' (p. 188) if currently under-represented groups are to achieve greater access to and success in Australian university life.

Indigenous Australians constitute the most disadvantaged group in Australian society, having significantly more health problems and significantly lower life expectancy than other Australians (Altman, Biddle, & Hunter, 2008). One key dimension of this marginalization is that 'Indigenous student participation, satisfaction and retention in higher education across Australia is abysmally low . . .' (Shah & Widin, 2010, p. 28). As a snapshot of Indigenous Australian university students' status, while there are welcome aspects of improvement and achievement, overall they remain far less likely than their non-Indigenous counterparts to succeed in their studies, and '. . . it is apparent that Australian universities have been struggling to attract and retain Indigenous students . . .' (p. 29). For instance, in 1998 Indigenous Australian university students constituted 1.2% (7,789) of all enrolments and 1.5% (3,997) of commencing enrolments, whereas 10 years later the proportions (and numbers) had declined to fewer than 1.0% (8,217) and 1.5% (3,351) respectively (p. 29). Also in 2008

Indigenous Australians made up 1.3% of Australian university students yet composed 2.2% of the Australian population (Bradley, Noonan, Nugent, & Scales, 2008).

Furthermore, current research reinforces the complexity of the phenomenon of university life for Indigenous Australians and the need to avoid homogenizing and essentializing their higher education experiences. For example, on the one hand, a large number of Indigenous Australians attending university have diagnosed mental health issues that require careful management (Toombs & Gorman, 2011). Moreover, a recent study of the perceptions of Indigenous students and staff members in a business degree (Fitzgerald, 2010) confirmed that 'A sense of community for Indigenous students was found [to be] lacking' (p. 19), and the proposals for action were centred on distinctively Indigenous identity issues: 'Recommendations include a cultural shift in the faculty towards engaging more deliberately with Indigenous topics in curriculum and research activities, expanding the enabling programme and strengthening relations with Indigenous high school students and communities' (p. 19).

On the other hand, in what was claimed to be '. . . the first in-depth analysis and benchmark model for development of success factors for retaining special entry [I]ndigenous Australian students in higher education' (Day & Nolde, 2009, p. 135), the findings were differentiated and somewhat unexpected:

> Positive or negative prior life experience had little impact on first year academic performance. Indigenous students as an equity group were found to have similar learning and life issues to non-[I]ndigenous students such as studying to improve job prospects and needing part-time employment to survive. They did not see themselves as different, and had no close relationship to [I]ndigenous knowledge or culture. Yet factors influencing academic success were related to [I]ndigeneity [,s]uch as close friendships and dependence on each other, mentoring care of staff, and rewards of fiving back through mentoring local [I]ndigenous school students. . . . Students adopted both [I]ndigenous and non-[I]ndigenous world perspectives and displayed robust resilience in the face of challenging family and educational experiences. (p. 135)

All of this represents a timely reminder that widening participation in Australian higher education is at once phenomenological and politicized, that its analyses and interpretations derive from competing theoretical and ideological frameworks, and that it is intimately connected with multiple manifestations of identities.

Who goes to university?

The Australian Commonwealth Government has provided a recent snapshot of university students in Australia (Australian Commonwealth Department of Education, Employment and Workplace Relations, 2010). In 2010 there were nearly 1.2 million students enrolled at Australian higher education providers, representing an increase of 5.1% over the previous year. Of that population, 72% were domestic students (an increase of 5.3% over 2009), and 28% were international students (in increase of 4.5% over 2009). More than two-thirds were studying full-time, and more than half (55.6%) were females.

Females also made up 56.2% of commencing students in Australian universities in 2010 (Australian Commonwealth Department of Education, Employment and Workplace Relations, 2010). Enabling (sometimes called bridging or preparatory) courses, defined as 'A course of instruction that enables a person to undertake a course leading to a higher education award', and sometimes constituting the most effective pathway for otherwise marginalized students to access higher education, increased nearly 20% over 2009.

Also in 2010, Indigenous Australians comprised 0.9% of all Australian university students (an increase of 6% over 2009) and 1.0% of commencing Australian university students (an increase of 4.9% over 2009). The subject areas in which most Indigenous Australians were enrolled included society and culture (32.7%), health (19.1%) and education (17.9%), although the percentages of total and commencing Indigenous Australians studying education declined over 2009 (Australian Commonwealth Department of Education, Employment and Workplace Relations, 2010).

Also in 2010, commencing Australian university students in 'regional' areas increased 11.0% over 2009 (to 63,461). In the same year, commencing students in 'remote' areas decreased 3.5% over 2009 (to 3,669 students) (Australian Commonwealth Department of Education, Employment and Workplace Relations, 2010).

Clearly, numbers and percentages of Australian university students in particular identified groups change from one data collection period to another. Longer-term trend data also vary, so that it is sometimes difficult to make a definitive case for particular groups' access and participation increasing or decreasing over time, and hence for the effectiveness or otherwise of specific strategies in contributing to such increases or decreases. With regard to the triple dimensions of the intersection between inequalities and identities in higher education – 'race', class and gender – with which this chapter is concerned, the outcome is mixed in current Australian university provision. Certainly females make up more than half the total and commencing student groups, although their representation in non-traditional subject areas such as engineering and science continues to be problematic. Socioeconomic status remains complex and contested as a site for generating productive and sustainable change; despite a large number of targeted initiatives, students from lower socioeconomic status backgrounds are still significantly less likely to enter, and then to remain in, higher education in Australia. This applies equally to Indigenous Australians, and also to other minority ethnic groups such as those from non-English-speaking backgrounds (Bowden & Doughney, 2010), Chinese international students (Xiao & Petraki, 2007) and African refugees in Australia (Harris & Marlowe, 2011).

The impact of tuition fees on higher education

As was noted above, in 1973 the Whitlam Labor Government abolished fees for Australian university students. These were reintroduced in 1989 by the next Labor Government, under Bob Hawke's prime ministership, in the form of HECS, '. . . an income contingent loan repayment scheme which the student can access' (Gregory, 2009, p. 238, note 2). In 1997, under the newly elected Coalition Government led by John Howard, the fees were increased and were '. . . differentiated into three cost bands, based on a combination of the relative cost of course delivery and the relative profitability (i.e., the rate of return) of certain programs' (Johnstone & Marcucci, 2010, p. 287), with medicine being in a higher band than teaching, for example. As at April 2012, the repayment thresholds and rates ranged from no repayment being required if the annual income were below $49,096 to 4% of the repayment income if that income were between $49,096 and $54,688 to 8% of the repayment income if that income were $91,178 and above (all figures in Australia dollars (Australian Taxation Office, 2012)).

Researchers vary widely in their views of the impact of HECS on the Australian university system broadly and on particular marginalized groups specifically. Gale (2009) links the scheme's introduction with the abolition of the binary system outlined above as '. . . help[ing] to fund the sector's expansion more generally' and as together constituting one of '. . . four expansion phases to date in the history of Australian higher education' (p. 3). Similarly, Johnstone and Marcucci (2010) note that, although '. . . HECS clearly shifted a significant portion of the higher educational cost burden from the government, or the Australian taxpayer, mainly onto students' (p. 4), 'Significantly, revenue to the Australian universities increased substantially; that is, the new tuition fees supplemented, rather than substituted for, government revenue, with no evident loss of enrollments or accessibility' (p. 4). Moreover, Marks (2009a) asserts that 'There is no evidence that socioeconomic inequalities in higher education in Australia increased after the implementation of HECS in 1989 or the 1997 reforms' (p. 71).

Interestingly, for many students HECS appears to be relatively low on the list of pressures and priorities confronting them, presumably because the scheme is income-contingent and can be deferred. For instance, in a recent study of diversity among Australian university students and how such diversity intersects with resilience and study progression (Kinnear, Boyce, Sparrow, Middleton, & Cullity, 2008), only 3% of factors identified by the 1,353 participating students as facilitating course progression related to 'Financial support (e.g., non-parental such as able to delay HECS, paid work)' (p. 28), whereas 43% referred to 'Support (from specific people such as financial motivation, assignments, living at home, encouragement, childcare, learning assistance)' (p. 28) and 21% applied to 'Self-characteristics (e.g., time management, organization, motivated, determined, hours spent studying)' (p. 28). In the same study, for the 50 participating staff members, these equivalent three factors of 'Financial support', 'Support (from others)' and 'Self-characteristics' or 'Personal-characteristics/behaviours' yielded 5%, 36% and 18% respectively, with staff members also generating 33% for 'Course-related issues (e.g., interesting content, learning/environments, flexibility, online resources, good tutors)' (p. 40), while students identified only 11% of factors being linked with 'Course-related issues'.

An additional consequence of the income-contingent character of HECS is what Australian economists Birch and Miller (2008) claim is its apparently only limited or '. . . modest effect, particularly among mature-age and part-time students . . . ' (p. 35). On the other hand, the byline for their article is, 'Blessed are the young, for they shall inherit a HECS debt' (p. 30), and they contend that '. . . the scheme has done little to improve the proportion of students from low socioeconomic backgrounds actually attending university' (p. 35). More seriously, they see a strong relationship between HECS and the perpetuation of socioeconomic status disparities:

> . . . students of a low socioeconomic status are considerably more likely to defer their HECS contribution than students of a higher socioeconomic status. Deferring HECS is associated with lower academic achievements during the first year of university. Moreover, students who defer their HECS liability have a lower likelihood of continuing their university study beyond the first year of university. . . . Finally, HECS debts have been linked to

changes in a range of post-graduation outcomes, including housing choice and earnings inequality, as it is typically measured. (p. 35)

Furthermore, particular groups of migrants living in Australia, such as Samoans, are unable to access HECS and so must pay university fees upfront; 'This is a prohibitive expense for most, so members of these families are generally denied higher education opportunities' (Zuber-Skerritt & Kearney, 2012, p. 172).

All of this highlights that, like so much else connected with international comparisons related to identity (and associated inequalities) and pedagogy in higher education, the financing of universities and student fees are highly differentiated phenomena that are deeply embedded in complex and dynamic contexts that simultaneously reflect diverse historical developments and contemporary global forces. This book seeks to contribute to ongoing and broader research into the lives of university students in both the UK and Australia who are variously marginalized, and into the intentions and impacts of government and institutional policies related to their educational experiences and outcomes.

NEETS

While the term 'NEETs' is generally not used in Australia (as it is in the UK) to denote young people not in education, employment or training, Australian governments are equally concerned to identify people who belong to this category and to develop strategies for engaging with them (Harreveld & Singh, 2009; Karmel & Liu, 2011).

There are significant disparities between the UK and Australia that reflect differences between their economies and business structures, as well as their educational systems. For example, '. . . fewer than one in ten employers in England offered apprenticeships in 2009, compared with a third of employers in Australia . . .' (Steedman, 2010, p. 2). Additionally, Australia tends to have longer periods of apprenticeships than England, which '. . . help[s] to offset the costs of such training for employers' (p. 2). At the same time, Australian researchers have noted the need to monitor and enhance the effectiveness of employment-based training if their learning outcomes are to be maximized (Choy, Bowman, Billett, Wignall, & Haukka, 2008).

The identification of 'NEETS' and the elaboration of policies to involve them in one or more of education, employment and training (and by implication to eliminate them as a social category) is often justified in terms of maximizing the social inclusion of marginalized and vulnerable individuals and groups. From a very different perspective, which conceptualizes '. . . social inclusion in human terms . . .' (Thomas & Hay, 2012, p. 141), there are concerns about policies reflecting '. . . a view of young people as a problem requiring government intervention' (p. 141). In particular:

> The policies sought to regulate young people and schooling through policy discourses that steered changes in the practices of senior secondary schooling. That is, the policy discourses realised spaces for the governance of schooling and young people as they constructed frameworks for actions aimed at increasing school retention and completion rates in order to build a skilled workforce to ensure economic prosperity. . . . This rationality constrained the practices available to young people, placing a heavy emphasis on linear progressions from school to post-school life. (p. 141)

It might be argued that paradoxically this specific approach to social inclusion is likely to homogenize the educational, employment and social experiences of young people and thus to reduce their sociocultural diversity.

The business of higher education?

As in the UK, so too is higher education increasingly subjected to the forces of marketization and globalization in Australia (see also Nickolai, Hoffman, & Trautner, 2012). As was noted above, Australia has followed the UK in implementing a Research Quality Framework exercise and currently an Excellence in Research in Australia initiative for predefined fields of research conducted by Australian universities. With the Excellence in Research in Australia activity, national audits have so far been conducted in 2010 and 2012. While it is too early to establish the influence of the outcomes on such issues as the Australian Government's distribution of research funding to individual universities, the audits' impact has certainly been felt in terms of the research and publishing approaches of academics, as well as in the bureaucratization and managerial corporatization of research and research management in Australian universities (see also Neumann & Guthrie, 2002).

Also like the UK, those same Australian universities have for a long time been involved in hosting students from other countries, a growing trend that also reflects the play of marketization and globalization and increased national and international competition for students (Marginson, 2011). This trend has had a continuing parallel effect on the international student recruitment practices of Australian universities (Ross, Grace, & Shao, 2012/in press) and on efforts to implement effective culturally inclusive practices in Australian universities (Wang, 2012). Certainly international students at Australian universities generate considerable income for the Australian economy. For example:

> In 2007 education exports, including spending by onshore students on tuition, housing, food, transport, living and entertainment, were A\$12.6 billion, 39 per cent from tuition.... [E]ducation was the third largest export (5.6 per cent) behind coal (9.5 per cent), iron ore (7.5 per cent) and ahead of tourism (5.4 per cent). In 2008 education exports reached A\$15.5 billion, up from \$8.6 billion in 2004. Education exports were at the level of 1.2 per cent of G[ross] D[omestic] P[roduct]. (Marginson, Nyland, Sawir, & Forbes-Mewett, 2010, p. 45)

Again like the UK, Australia exhibits many of the elements of the continuing commodification of higher education. This has been seen, for instance, in diverse and competing ideological framings of notions of equitable access, success and quality for Australian university students (Gidley, Hampson, Wheeler, & Bereded-Samuel, 2010). It has also been manifested in policies driving changes to universities evidencing such themes as a 'techno-scientific orientation, network characteristics and commercial imperatives' (Kenway, Bullen, & Robb, 2004, p. 330). And it has definitely been experienced in the significantly shifting professional roles and responsibilities of Australian academics (Santoro & Snead, 2012/in press) and in the changing patterns of university governance (Rowlands, 2012/in press).

This chapter has presented a comparative account of selected elements of the higher education contexts in the UK and Australia, as a backdrop to understanding how multiple student identities are framed and reframed in those contexts. Discussion of those identities focused on some of the ways in which inequalities are replicated and/or ameliorated by means of participation in university education. Such inequalities include 'race' or ethnicity, class or socioeconomic status and gender. Identity (re)construction in relation to these markers of difference influences, and in turn is influenced by, the respective higher education systems in the two countries, and it is the similarities and differences in the historical development and contemporary enactment of these systems that help to explain equivalent similarities and differences in the university experiences of particular marginalized groups in each country.

Note

1 HEFCE distributes public money to universities and colleges in England that provide higher education. The council distributes money to universities and colleges for higher education teaching, research and related activities. Its main aims are to fund programmes to support the development of higher education, to monitor the financial aspect of how universities spend their money, to ensure the quality of teaching and to provide guidance on 'good practice' in higher education.

Educational Identities in the UK and Australia

Chapter 2 highlighted a number of contemporary theoretical and empirical debates, all connected with crucial elements of educational identities. Chapter 3 articulated some of the complex links between such identities and higher education in the UK and Australia.

This chapter builds on that discussion by exploring at greater depth the concepts of Whiteness and Blackness and discusses these within the contexts of formal education in the UK and Australia (with comparative references where relevant to the situation in the USA).

More specifically, the chapter examines the work of Ware and Back (2001), Frankenberg (1993, 1997), David Gillborn (2008, 2009) and Zeus Leonardo (2002, 2005, 2009), as well as the scholarship of Black Feminists such as Hill Collins (1990) and Mirza (1992, 2009). It analyses how identities are constructed within the frameworks of culture and belonging in relation to being White and Black. We draw on previous literature that has explored issues of identity from this perspective and provide a critical interrogation of the debates and issues as well as an analysis of how those debates are situated within the wider purview of the academy.

White educational identities

Whiteness as an identity

The concept of Whiteness has received considerable attention in recent decades. Early work on Whiteness focused on examining Whiteness as a specific ethnic and racial identity (which was previously not discussed). The study of Whiteness has become a focus of concern for sociologists (Nayak, 2003), geographers (Bonnett, 2000; Winders, 2003) and educationalists alike (Preston, 2000). Those interested in education have focused on CRT as an understanding of Whiteness and its relationship to educational inequalities with regard to the experiences of BME groups (Delgado, 1995; Gillborn, 2008; Leonardo, 2009) (that understanding is elaborated later in this section of the chapter). In the USA, studies on Whiteness have tended to focus on groups described as 'White trash' (Jarosz & Lawson, 2002) and the underclass (Massey, 2007), whereas in the UK, similar studies have highlighted the experiences of White marginalized groups such as Gypsies and Travellers (Haylett, 2005; Turner, 2000). In Australia, scholarship has emphasized the previous supposed invisibility of Whiteness (Pugliese & Stryker, 2009) compared with the racialized visibility, not only of Indigenous Australians (Banerjee & Tedmanson, 2010), but also of particular groups of migrants such as Black Africans (Mapedzahama, Rudge, West, & Perron, 2012), Cypriot Turkish (Ali & Sonn, 2009, 2010), Turkish and South and Central Americans (Zevallos, 2008), and asylum seekers (Every & Augoustinos, 2008; Tascón, 2008) (see also Dunn, Forrest, Pe-Pua, Hynes, & Maeder-Han, 2009).

Whiteness in the USA

Historical work on Whiteness has been mapped out by historians in the USA (Ignatiev, 1995; Jacobson, 1998; Roediger, 1994). Noel Ignatiev is best known for his journal *Race Traitor*, and for calling for the abolition of the White race, which he contends is based on 'White privilege and race identity'. His seminal work, *How the Irish became White* (1995), examines the process by which the Irish became identified as White. He does so by analysing the concept of Whiteness in relation to the assimilation of the Irish into US culture and society. His main argument focuses on the acceptance of the Irish White identity owing to their contribution to the labour market. Roediger in the *Wages of Whiteness* (1992) and *Towards the abolition of Whiteness* (1994) examines how Whiteness is a symbol of power and status.

The work of Ruth Frankenberg (1993) nearly two decades ago was influential in opening up debates about the discourses of Whiteness and its relationship to structures of power and inequality. Frankenberg defines the concept of Whiteness by examining it from three specific dimensions:

> Whiteness is a location of structural advantage, of race privilege; it is a 'standpoint', a place from which White people look at ourselves, at others

and at society. Whiteness refers to a set of cultural practices that are usually unmarked and unnamed. (1993, p. 1)

From this perspective, Frankenberg (1993) notes that the identity of Whiteness is associated with a position of dominance; that is to say, Whiteness as a concept has to be understood in relation to discourses associated with dimensions of power in terms of racism. What is particularly interesting about Frankenberg's work is how she relates the concept of Whiteness to historical *change* in which its definition can change, at different times and at different places: 'Whiteness changes over time and space. . . . It is a complexly constructed product of local, regional, national and global relations, past and present' (1993, p. 236). Whiteness is thus seen as a contested concept related to discourses around 'race', racism and power (Dyer, 1997; Frankenberg, 1997; Ware & Black, 2002).

Hartigan's (1997) work has used the concept of Whiteness to examine the position of poor White working-class groups in Detroit. In his research he analyses how, even though some groups are identified as being White, they do not in fact enjoy the same privileges as other White (more privileged, affluent and middle class) groups. He compares the situation for suburban White groups with that of poor disadvantaged White groups and concludes that the treatment received by poor White groups is very different to that received by suburban Whites. In some cases, poor Whites are treated in the same ways as Black groups who experience racism and oppression: 'Whites in this neighbourhood did not participate in the same order of racial privilege and power with which Whiteness is typically associated' (p. 187). As Hartigan states:

> The meaning of race varies from location to location, but it also depends on the set of concerns against which it is prioritized and the other forms of consciousness or modes of reading with which it is ranked and arranged. (p. 188)

The poor Whites or 'White trash' in Hartigan's study are clearly not advantaged in any way; rather, they experience great disadvantages owing to their position in society.

Some researchers have examined the identity and concept of Whiteness in terms of how it is associated with issues of space. While Kobayashi and Peake (2000) argue that Whiteness is associated with privilege and power, they also state that the identity of *being White* is associated with space, and that racialization is '. . . the process by which racialized groups are identified, given stereotypical characteristics, and coerced into specific living conditions, often

involving social/spatial segregation and always constituting radicalized places'
(p. 393). Their understanding of Whiteness is based on Whites having the power
to enjoy particular advantages and privileges, 'by controlling dominant values
and institutions and, in particular, by *occupying space* within a segregated social
landscape' (p. 393; *italics in original*). Furthermore, they assert that 'Racism also
involves the manipulation of power to mark "White" as a location of social
privilege' (p. 394).

Hill's work (2008) provides a specifically US-based understanding of the
concept of Whiteness. She argues that White racist culture is shaped by a 'White
racial frame', an organized set of racialized ideas, stereotypes, emotions and
inclinations to discriminate (Feagin, 2006, p. 27, as cited in Hill, 2008, p. 4).
She focuses on how cultures of racism in the USA are produced and further
reproduced through the use of language in the media, literary texts and everyday
conversation. She relates this to an understanding of 'White virtue' – the idea that
the position occupied by White groups is highest in the hierarchy, because they
have the qualities that enable them to hold such a position. She uses the example
of residential segregation to demonstrate how White privilege works and how
White privilege is constructed. She states that '. . . residential segregation also
illustrates how White racist culture can be perpetuated in a sort of closed loop of
feedback as Whites gain credit and people of colour are discredited through this
practice' (p. 24). Her analysis of the use of language to demonstrate the relative
positions of White power and Black disadvantage includes the use of slurs in
speech. The use of such slurs in language enables and encourages individuals to
talk about 'race' and racism in a public and everyday manner.

This key element of Whiteness in the USA is further demonstrated by research
that has shown that the use of racist language is commonplace among college
and university campuses there (Delgado & Stefanic, 2000; Myers, 2005). See for
example how the highly offensive word 'nigger' and its connotations have been
used in the USA and the UK and how different discourses are used within it
(Kennedy, 2002). Hill's work demonstrates that language itself can be seen as a
powerful marker of difference in which covert racist discourses are used, 'with
a way of speaking that Whites do not understand as racist, but which works to
reproduce negative stereotypes of people of colour' (p. 119).

Whiteness in the UK

Bonnett (2000) in a UK analysis examines how Whiteness became an identity
that was available to the White working class, 'because of changes within the

socioeconomic and symbolic structuring of British capitalism' (p. 30). According to Bonnett, these changes were based on '. . . a shift in emphasis from Whiteness as a bourgeois identity, connoting extraordinary qualities, to Whiteness as a popularist identity connoting superiority but also ordinariness, nation and community' (p. 30).

Bonnett (2000) analyses the concept of Whiteness in terms of imperial and colonial understandings in the USA relating to how discourses and identities of Whiteness have been denied to groups such as Irish and Italian immigrants who were socially and economically excluded from Anglo-American society. Bonnett draws on the seminal work of Ignatiev (1995) to argue that a process of exclusion through to inclusion has taken place in which Irish immigrants gradually became accepted into US society because of their economic contributions and power in the labour market. White Irish groups were seen initially as 'outsiders' and 'others', owing to their 'persistent cultural representation as non-civilized and primitive' (pp. 22–3). According to Bonnet with regard to the situation of White identities in the UK, he argues that the notion of a 'White identity' became prevalent only when immigration was introduced and consequently there was competition for jobs and housing. The idea of Whiteness was attributed only to the middle classes, and White working-class groups were not seen as White enough or not quite White. Indeed, Whiteness in this sense was seen as 'a supremacist identity' (p. 40).

What much of the research demonstrates is that the identity of being White does not automatically equate to privilege, advantage and success. Haylett's research (2001) demonstrates that Whiteness is based on sociocultural, economic and psychological processes at work. This is also related to acceptable and non-acceptable shades of Whiteness as forms of identity and discourse (Bonnett, 1998; Wray & Newitz, 1997). Such acceptable and non-acceptable shades of Whiteness construct such groups as the 'other'. The research has also highlighted how some White groups continue to experience racism in relation to their status as White outsiders (such as Gypsies and Travellers) (see Bhopal & Myers, 2008; Neal, 2002; Ray & Read, 2005). As Haylett (2005) states:

> Whilst being legally recognized as an ethnic minority in Britain, Gypsy Travellers themselves have an ambiguous relationship to Whiteness. On the one hand, they are not necessarily a visible minority easily distinguishable from the rest of the (heterogeneous) White population; on the other hand the boundaries of Whiteness are not always defined to embrace this group. (p. 353)

Whiteness in Australia

A similar complexity and diversity attend scholarly analyses of Whiteness in contemporary Australia. Conflicting understandings of the constituent elements of 'ethnicities' and 'national identities' – including Whiteness and 'Australianness' – certainly underpinned the 'Cronulla riots' between White and Muslim Australians in Sydney in 2005 (Bliuc, McGarty, Hartley, & Muntele Hendres, 2012/in press), for example. Similarly varied conceptions of, and anxieties about, Whiteness have been claimed to underlie the discourses and practices of Australian vocational educators and their students (Shore, 2010). Not surprisingly, the many current enactments of Whiteness as an ideology have been traced to the development of powerful ideas in Australia's colonial and supposedly postcolonial past (Carey & McLisky, 2009).

As in the USA and the UK, Whiteness in Australia functions as a powerful economic, political and sociocultural force. For instance, Matereke states baldly that '. . . "being Australian" is a tool for both inclusion and exclusion in Australia', and that '. . . discourses of white hegemony' contrive to position '. . . the normalisation of whiteness as the essence of "Australianness"' (p. 129). From a different perspective, social work as a discipline of study in Australian universities (and as a professional practice intended to contribute to advancing the welfare of marginalized communities) has been critiqued as exhibiting a '. . . Euro-centric heritage with its often taken-for granted knowledges and principles which negatively affect Indigenous peoples' and that often generate '. . . ongoing and largely un-reflexive practices . . .' (Young & Zubrzycki, 2011, p. 159). Moreover, often unexamined notions and experiences of Australian Whiteness are deeply embedded and intricately interwoven in cultural artefacts such as films (Williams, 2009) and art, cartoons, literature and music (Anscombe, 2010).

Several of these multiple and overlapping elements of Australian Whiteness have been usefully synthesized by Koerner (2011):

> . . . Australia has protected its white sovereignty through four key points. First, . . . the Australian nation has been produced as a racialised entity with whiteness as the hegemonic norm . . . which shapes white power and privileged in Australia; second . . . multiculturalism in Australia has been used as a framework to deal with difference within which race is obscured; third . . . white Australian discourses of nation and identity are limited in their ability to be located in Indigenous sovereignty; and finally, . . . discourses of multiculturalism and Indigenous sovereignty are rarely addressed in a coherent manner . . . (p. 1)

Thus Australian Whiteness is as extensive and powerful as it is complex and diverse – and as it is in the USA and the UK. Despite growing and ongoing scholarly attention, it remains influential partly because it continues to exhibit apparent invisibility. Yet that seeming invisibility has been subjected to increased interrogation, not least by means of explicating its multiple connections with and disconnections from Blackness and Black educational identities.

Black educational identities

Blackness as an identity

Writers such as Gilroy (1987) and Modood (1988) have argued that when discussing terms such as 'Black', 'Asian' or 'White' it is important to consider discourses around the terms that are not politically neutral or even static. The use of the nomenclature here is important as it encourages political reflexivity as well as using terms that may be reductive (see also Bonnett, 2000). In the UK there has been a great deal of controversy surrounding the usage of terms to define who is Black and who is not. Quite often these controversies have been introduced by the people themselves who have been labelled as either Black or Asian.

As a striking illustration of the disputatious character and long-term personal and collective impact of these kinds of debates, Kalwant Bhopal, the first-named author of this book, presents the following recollection:

I would like to offer a small incident that occurred while I was an undergraduate student at a 'new' (post-1992) university in London, UK in the late 1980s. As a first year undergraduate, I was becoming increasingly aware of my own identity as a British Asian woman within a political context. A Black (Afro-Caribbean) female friend and I decided to attend the 'Black Students Forum' together. This was a group that had created a Black space for students to discuss issues that concerned them around racism and how Black students could 'make a difference' to higher education. As we entered the room, I did not notice at the time that it was full of African-Caribbean students and I was the only Asian student present. The two students – one male and one female – who were introducing and chairing the event explained that the 'Black Students Forum' was set up because many of the Black students did not feel that they had a space in which they could share their experiences of *being Black*. The female student said that it would be a good point of introductory discussion to examine what the term 'Black' meant and whom it applied to.

At this point, a young Black male student said that he thought that being Black was associated with a history of oppression that included racism and slavery. He then pointed to me and said, 'She's not Black and I don't think she should be here'. At this point, I was horrified and also quite shocked and upset by this incident. In my mind, I did not see myself as anything other than being non-White. I saw myself as Black as a political identity, rather than as a personal identity (although my position has now changed somewhat). Needless to say, I walked out and never returned to the 'Black Students Forum'. I am sure that many Black people do not see Asian people as having a Black identity, precisely because of the different experiences that the two groups have. But both groups experience racism on a regular basis, and it is from this premise that many non-White people *unite* in their oppression, rather than use difference to divide them.

Blackness in the USA

Blackness continues to constitute a highly ambiguous and ambivalent, yet also influential and ubiquitous, set of ideas on the USA. For instance, a recent analysis of Black superheroes in children's comics (Nama, 2011; see also Soto & Showers Johnson, 2011) reveals that Black identities stand at the crossroads of broader and highly '. . . significant cultural dynamics, social trends, and historical events' (p. 3). As another example, the Black Power Movement emerged as strong political identity – in the USA as well as in other countries – that focused on the identities of being Black and the African Diaspora (Rabier, Hintzen, & Smith, 2010). There is also the commercialized and often politicized position occupied by Black athletes in highly lucrative sports such as professional basketball (Yep, 2012) and tennis (Douglas, 2012).

This same ambiguity and ambivalence about the character and meanings of Blackness traverse a wide range of other fields of public and private activity. These include presidential and gubernatorial election campaigns (James, 2010), marketing and advertising (Crockett, 2008), contemporary literature (Sabatini Sloan, 2010), disability studies (Bell, 2011) and educational leadership (Horsford & Tillman, 2012). In each of these can be traced the anxieties, aspirations, tensions and occasional triumphs attendant on the interplay of identities and the performativity of subjectivities against the backdrop of wider economic, political and sociocultural forces and influences.

Blackness in the UK

Those African-Caribbeans and Asians who migrated to the UK in the post-war period occupied similar positions in society, both in the labour market and in the economy. At the time, the term 'coloured people' was used to describe them. These groups suffered overt discrimination in the labour market, housing, education and society in general, simply by being non-White. More recently, the term 'Black' has been used to describe those from minority ethnic communities and has increasingly emerged as a political rather than a personal term.

Mercer (1994) argues that the concept of Black in the UK emerged in response to, and as a reaction to, categories such as 'immigrant' and 'ethnic minority'. The use of the term 'Black' was criticized for referring only to the struggles encountered and recognized by those of African heritage and descent and for not applying to the experiences of those of South Asian origin. In this sense, the category 'Black' was seen as political and one that denied the existence of an Asian cultural identity (Hazareesingh, 1986; Modood, 1988). As Brah (1996) has argued, 'Given that cultural processes are dynamic and the process of claiming is itself mediated, the term "Black" does not have to be construed in essentialist terms. It can have different political and cultural meanings in different contexts' (p. 98).

On the other hand, using the term 'Black' can deny cultural differences and specifics between groups who have diverse cultural experiences and identities. Furthermore, many South Asians would not define themselves as Black (Bhopal, 2010) and many Black people would not recognize Asian people as having a Black identity (as was demonstrated in the personal example outlined above). Furthermore, some Asian groups might define themselves in relation to experiencing racism but might still differentiate themselves from Black groups owing to their own cultural norms, practices and heritage.

Brah (1996) argues that the term 'Black' conceals the cultural needs of groups, but focuses instead on the needs of those of African-Caribbean origin. Here she uses the concept of ethnicism to argue that the experiences of racialized groups are seen in culturalist terms – that is, with regard only to their ethnic differences. Others have contended that the term 'Black' is limited as it is often used for the formation of social policy and the allocation of resources (Gillborn, 2005; Gilroy, 1987). Consequently, the term 'Black' that was once used to promote solidarity between non-White groups has in some sense become one that divides African-Caribbean and South Asian groups as they compete for jobs, housing and resources. This is even more pertinent in the current economic climate in the

UK in which it has been argued that the recent recession could affect attitudes to 'race' and minority ethnic groups as individuals compete for jobs and housing (*Daily Telegraph*, 2009).

Hazareesingh (1986) and Modood (1988) have both argued that the concept of Black should be used to refer only to those of African-Caribbean heritage. Hazareesingh (1986) has suggested that the term 'Indian' be used to describe those from South Asian origin. However, those from South Asia have a diverse range of cultures and identifiers so the concept of Indian would be inaccurate. Modood (1988), on the other hand, would prefer to use the term 'Asian' rather than 'Black', and furthermore he dismisses the term 'South Asian' as an academic term. By contrast, Brah (1996) has contended that this creates additional problems as Modood (1988) refers to the heritage of Hindustan prior to the British conquest.

What is clear here is the different usages of key terms concerned with identities are located at the intersection of longstanding and enduring historical and political processes. More recent research has shown that many Asian women define themselves as British Indian or Asian British and that relatively few refer to themselves as Black, partly as a response to racist experiences in the UK (Bhopal, 2010). Modood (2007) has argued that we should be careful when establishing binaries of 'Black/White' when considering research on 'race' and identity.

Blackness in Australia

As in the USA and the UK, Blackness assumes diverse designs and multiple manifestations in Australia. There are the unexpected overlaps and contradictions between Blackness and gender, for instance, such as those experienced in interracial relationships (Blanch, 2012/in press), and between Blackness and sexuality as highlighted in audience responses to an Australia tele-series called *The Circuit* (Crowley & Rasmussen, 2010). There are the equally complicated intersections between Blackness and socioeconomic status, as exemplified by the often tense interactions between urban Indigenous Australians and newly resettled African refugees (Colic-Peisker & Tilbury, 2008). And there are the potentially life-threatening misunderstandings and competing constructions of Aboriginality between Indigenous Australian patients and non-Indigenous living and working in remote Indigenous Australian communities (Saethre, 2009).

At the same time, there are other and more enabling and positive enactments of Blackness in Australia. For example, there is the exploration of the mutual insights into two very different cultural systems to be gleaned from performing Shakespeare and Aboriginality (Cox, 2011). Moreover, there is a great deal of evidence of Indigenous Australians both historically and currently deploying considerable resilience and resistance in their interactions with the British invaders. A striking example is the ways in which the Anangu people living in the eastern part of the Western Desert in Australia '. . . eagerly appropriated . . . [m]aterial colours, . . . which] have become integral to Anangu's conception of their own humanity in the contemporary world' (Young, 2011, p. 356). Furthermore, Indigenous Australian community leaders are recognized by at least some commentators as comprising intellectuals with highly developed capabilities and skills of communication, reflection and understanding (Moses, 2010), despite the pressures consequent on their leading '. . . a tiny minority in a settler society . . .' (p. 9).

Whiteness, Blackness and Critical Race Theory

CRT grew out of legal studies in the USA. It works on the premise that racism exists in society, at all times and in all places. This is racism ranging from its obvious form as heard in overt name calling to the more covert, hidden and underlying versions present in everyday structures of power. Some terms used in relation to CRT include interest-convergence (Bell, 1980) in which it is argued that White people will stand up for the rights of Black people only if these interests work for the White people rather than for the Blacks – that is, for self-interest and self-gain.

Many writers examining the concept of Whiteness have used it to apply to notions of CRT and also to propositions of White supremacy. Both Zeus Leonardo and David Gillborn in their recent works analyse Whiteness in relation to White racial domination. For example, ' . . . a critical look at White privilege, or the analysis of White racial hegemony, must be complemented by an equally rigorous examination of White supremacy, or the analysis of White racial domination' (Leonardo, 2009, p. 75). Leonardo argues that simply by being White gives White people a privilege that means that they are treated better than Blacks in all aspects of their lives, particularly in relation to housing, education and immigration laws in the USA. The idea of Whiteness being a superior identity to those from minority ethnic backgrounds is related to historical notions of slavery, segregation and discrimination and this is particularly relevant to the USA. For Leonardo, 'Whiteness is a racial discourse, whereas the category "White

people" represents a socially constructed identity, usually based on skin colour'
(2009, p. 169).

Gillborn (2010) also uses the concept of White supremacy and applies it to an
understanding of interest-convergence (Bell, 1980) in relation to CRT:

> CRT does not imagine that all White people are uniformly racist and
> privileged. However, CRT *does* view all White-identified people as implicated
> in relations of White domination. White people do not all behave in identical
> ways and they do not draw similar benefits – but they *do* all benefit to some
> degree, whether they like it or not. (p. 4; *italics in original*)

Gillborn's (2010) use of the concept White supremacy is therefore based on the
notion that the interests of White people are always privileged and this behaviour
is seen as the norm and consequently not questioned. In relation to class and
poverty, Gillborn contends that it is not only privileged Whites who benefit from
a White status but also poor working-class Whites who benefit, but they do so
in different ways:

> Race and class intersect so that, under certain conditions, both middle class
> and working class Whites benefit from a shared White identity. Indeed, it can
> be argued *that the existence of poor Whites is not only consistent with White
> supremacy, it is actually an essential part of the processes that sustain it.* (p. 6;
> *italics in original*)

Gillborn (2005) has further asserted that education policy itself can be seen as
an act of White supremacy. Leonardo (2009) contends that '. . . *all Whites benefit
from race racism, but they do not all benefit equally from other social relations*' (p.
121; *italics in original*). This is further demonstrated by McIntosh (1992), who
identifies White privilege as being a bag full of goodies to which only White
people have access. These goodies are unrecognized advantages that they carry
in their daily lives, such as '. . . assurances, tools, guides, codebooks, passports,
visas . . .' (p. 291) and so on.

Within education the use of CRT has been powerfully analysed by Gloria
Ladson-Billings (2009) and William Tate (1997), particularly in relation to
how 'race' is seen as a marker of difference and underachievement (Gillborn,
2008; Ladson-Billings, 2009). This has been demonstrated in empirical research
in which 'race' acts as a discriminatory marker in educational tests and the
measurement of achievement (Au, 2009; Gillborn & Youdell, 2000). Michael
Apple's work has been highly influential in how 'race' is constructed and marked
out as the 'other' (Apple, 2006).

Ladson-Billings (2009) in her work examines how CRT can be used to inform citizenship studies and how particular subjects are taught in line with social justice and inclusion principles, as well as how school funding is distributed.

The work of CRT has been used to interrogate how racism operates within educational discourses and how barriers to educational equity can be addressed for those from non-White backgrounds. Marxist understandings of CRT in the UK have pointed to the problematizing of the centrality of 'race' in CRT and a critique of White supremacy (Cole, 2009; Cole & Stuart, 2005), as well as the application of CRT from the USA to the UK contexts (Cole & Maisuria, 2010). And it has also been deployed effectively by an Australian classroom teacher (Vass, 2012/in press) to identify '. . . the racialised underpinnings of the Australian educational setting' and to assist with '. . . enhancing understanding of Indigenous schooling and contemporary educational research'.

Whiteness, Blackness and education

With regard to formal education and pedagogy, it has been argued that students should think about issues of Whiteness in relation to their own identity as a means of developing a critical pedagogy of Whiteness. One of the issues associated with teaching Whiteness includes the need to identify and make sense of 'White power' and 'White privilege' (Kincheloe & Steinberg, 1998). Moreover, Kincheloe and Steinberg (1988) state that '. . . White students from middle/upper class backgrounds frequently resist a pedagogy of Whiteness as a threat to their privilege' (p. 18). Part of this process is the unlearning of racism and developing an awareness of what it means to share interests with those from non-White backgrounds. Rodriguez (1998) further argues that to think of a pedagogy of Whiteness must also include adopting a critical perspective on what that means, particularly when dealing with Whiteness and issues of power relations.

bell hooks (1992) states that all Black people critically examine the White identity and notions of Whiteness. She argues that all Black people in the USA (regardless of their social class and background) will always feel threatened by White people. She contends that, when White students are told these things, they '. . . respond with naïve amazement that Black people critically assess White people from a standpoint where Whiteness is the privileged signifier' (p. 339). So Whiteness is rarely questioned, particularly by White students. As hooks asserts, this is because Black people generally remain silent about their feelings about Whiteness and in some sense pretend to be comfortable in relation to discourses around Whiteness, but in reality Whiteness is seen as 'terrorising' (p. 341). Whiteness is associated with goodness and Blackness is associated with being bad:

> Socialized to believe the fantasy that whiteness represents goodness and all that is benign and non-threatening, many white people assume this is the way that black people conceptualize whiteness. They do not imagine that the way whiteness makes its presence felt in black life, most often as terrorizing imposition, a power that wounds, hurts, tortures, is a reality that disrupts the fantasy of whiteness as representing goodness. (pp. 340–1)

In the USA, Leonardo (2009) also examines educational policy-making as 'an act of Whiteness' (p. 127). In particular, he argues that the *No Child Left Behind* Act (which is very similar to the Every Child Matters Agenda in the UK) 'perpetuates the innocence of Whiteness as a system of privilege' (p. 127). Such policies are based on the premise that discourses of Whiteness derive from systems of White privilege in which policies reinforce and uphold the superior status of Whites, and consequently the *No Child Left Behind* policy helps to construct the notion of 'White nationhood' (p. 128).

Tatum (2009) contends that to teach White students about discourses of racism is related to how we tackle issues of Whiteness. Teaching White and Black students about racism should include how individuals have been victimized by oppression, as well as how they resist such oppression. White students should be taught that they must speak up against racism and oppression, and challenge others to do the same:

> Teaching about racism needs to shift from an exploration of the experiences of victims and victimizers to that of empowered people of colour and their White allies, creating the possibility of working together as partners in the establishment of a more just society. (p. 287)

The work of John Preston (2007) has explored the intersections of Whiteness and class in education and the formation of White identities in relation to White privilege.

Preston (2007) examines how Whiteness and class are articulated in educational settings, particularly in relation to further education colleges. He uses a Bourdieuian analysis of class to analyse the relationship between 'the interplay and exchange of capitals, strategies of recognition and mis-recognition and distinction' (p. 13).

A great deal of scholarship has examined how educational institutions disregard issues of 'race' and Whiteness, specifically in relation to the educational habitus of Black and White working-class students (Archer & Leathwood, 2003). Research by Leathwood and Hutchings (2003) examines how class, gender and 'race' affect how students are allocated particular options in further education colleges. This in turn influences the type of university and course that such students may attend and complete. Preston's (2007) focus on class analysis in relation to Whiteness and education shows that 'Class is relevant to all of this analysis but whilst class fragments Whiteness it does not alter "White supremacy" which is a key analytical tool for the future interrogation of educational policy or practice' (p. 189).

At the same time, much of the contemporary literature has focused on the complicated relationship between formal education and Blackness. This relationship is evident, for instance, in significantly varied attitudes among community leaders to race relations and educational provision in Brazil (Baiocchi & Corrado, 2010). Similarly, constructions of Blackness (and of Whiteness) can be distilled from popular culture, but adult educators need support and training in undertaking such a distillation (Wright & Sandin, 2009). And a key implication on the previous hegemony of Whiteness in analyses of education is that there are new and powerful stories to be told and written about Black and other minority ethnic experiences in recounting and recuperating the histories of education to take account of these previously unheard voices (Myers, 2009).

Much of the research in the USA, the UK and Australia reported in this chapter has focused on issues of identity, diversity and diaspora, particularly by examining what it means to be White and what it means to be Black. A critical understanding of these identities arose from a political perspective, specifically around discrimination and oppression. These perspectives were used to understand how minority ethnic groups were able to position themselves (and how they were positioned) in relation to those from White backgrounds. The chapter also distilled important educational dimensions of these White and Black identities, not least because formal education occupies a key yet contradictory position in this book. On the one hand, it functions in many ways to replicate and perpetuate the kinds of marginalizing experiences recorded in the chapter. On the other hand, it represents the best chance for creating alternative and more transformative life chances for all learners, whether White or Black. However, as the next two chapters demonstrate, formal education, as encapsulated by higher education, presents a mixed picture in terms of creating the conditions for this kind of transformation in the UK and Australia.

5

Researching Racialized Identities

This chapter outlines the research context by exploring the methods that were used in the empirical research analysed in the next chapter, as well as the authors' respective and in some ways reversed experiences as researchers: the first-named author's position as a Black woman in conducting research in the UK, and the second-named author's perspective as a White man in conducting research in Australia. The chapter explores the effects of 'race', gender, power and class on the research process, and also discusses issues of access. The chapter examines how the research was situated in two differing contexts socially and politically – the UK and Australia – and how such contexts affect our understandings of identity and pedagogy within higher education.

Research in the UK

The research in England was commissioned by Multiverse[1] in 2008 to examine understandings of 'race', diversity and inclusion in a largely White university located on the south coast of England. The university was selected because of its numbers of predominantly White students in primary and secondary PGCE courses. The PGCE in England exists for students who already have a degree and want to train as teachers (either in primary or in secondary schools). A PGCE course focuses mainly on developing teaching skills, and not on the subject that students intend to teach. For this reason, students are expected to have a good understanding of their chosen subject(s) – usually to degree level – before they start their training. Students are also required to have a standard equivalent to a grade C in GCSE[2] English and mathematics. If students want to teach primary or key stage 2/3 (ages 7–14), they must also have achieved a standard equivalent to a grade C in a science GCSE. At the time of writing, funding was available for students wanting to study for a PGCE in England, Wales and Scotland.

The main aims of the study were to explore trainee teachers' (and tutors') understandings of issues centred on 'race', diversity and educational inclusion. The understandings of a predominantly White trainee teacher intake were a particular emphasis and were reflected in the research objectives of the study. These were focused mainly on the issues that trainee teachers felt were important in teaching 'race', diversity and inclusion as well as on exploring the kinds of materials that could be used to benefit trainee teachers and tutors to understand these issues more fully in the classroom (for a detailed discussion of this see Bhopal, Harris, & Rhamie, 2009). The research also charted constructions of identity by students and tutors; we were particularly concerned to examine how they understood their own ethnic identities in relation to being teachers and practising in the classroom. The focus was also on how the concepts of diversity and inclusion were understood and how these were likely to reflect their future teaching. As was noted above, selected findings of this research are presented in the next chapter.

Methodology

The research took place in two stages. In stage one, a total of 59 questionnaire surveys were distributed to PGCE students for one academic intake and a further 45 were distributed for a different academic intake, totalling 104 student teachers who participated in the survey. The majority of respondents who filled in the questionnaires were on secondary PGCE courses, with only 27 on primary PGCE courses. Stage two of the research consisted of in-depth qualitative interviews with students. Ten interviews were carried out with the first academic intake of students and twenty were carried out with the second intake of students. Questionnaires were distributed to students during class time by tutors who were teaching on the PGCE course. All respondents were asked to fill in a consent form and the research project adhered to the research requirements as outlined in the British Educational Research Association and the British Sociological Association ethical guidelines. Respondents were also assured of anonymity and confidentiality and were told that they did not have to participate in the research. All of the interviews were tape recorded and later transcribed. Permission was obtained from respondents to use their interview material for publication; all respondents agreed for their interviews to be used in this way.

As we were interested as well in examining tutors' understanding of 'race', diversity and inclusion, we also asked tutors to participate in the research. Questionnaires for tutors were distributed via pigeon holes and tutors were asked to fill in questionnaires anonymously. Twenty questionnaires were distributed to tutors, but only five responded and only two tutors agreed to participate in interviews. One of the reasons for this may have been due to the sensitive nature of the research project as well as respondents having a perceived or potential conflict of interest, as they were currently teaching in the institution in which the research was taking place and where the researcher was also a member of staff. As a result of this lack of response, we decided to conduct interviews in a similar university (in terms of student/staff ethnic make-up). We were able to conduct ten interviews with tutors in this other institution, where there was no conflict of interest for the tutors.

Both of the universities in which the research took place are 'red brick', prestigious and well-established universities. The first university is part of the Worldwide Universities Network. It currently has over 17,000 undergraduates and 7,000 postgraduates enrolled in courses; as a result it is one of the largest universities in the South East of England. Both universities have a strong emphasis on research and are regarded as centres for excellence and rank highly in national and international university league tables.

Methodological difficulties

Gaining access

Once ethical clearance had been obtained from the university ethics committee, permission was obtained from the programme leader for primary and secondary PGCE courses. Gaining access to students on the PGCE courses for this project did not prove to be problematic as one of the researchers was employed at one of the universities. Tutors were contacted and asked if they would distribute questionnaires to their students. We emphasized that tutors should make it clear to students that they did not have to participate and were not under any pressure to do so. The participation and response rates for student questionnaires were good; however, relatively few agreed to be interviewed.

There are clearly disadvantages associated with conducting research in institutions in which the researchers are employed. We did feel that perhaps some of the students did not wish to be interviewed as they knew one of the researchers involved in the project. Furthermore, this may have been one of the reasons why tutors chose not to participate in the project. These issues of access are related to power differentials in the research relationship remaining unbalanced in the interests of the researcher (who usually has the most power) rather than in the interests of the respondent (who usually has less power). Some of the questions related to issues of access included: to what extent students and tutors felt that they were pressured to participate in the research, as well as the extent to which students felt that their participation in the research would affect their performance in the PGCE course. Such issues had to be considered when researching with those in less powerful positions than the researchers, and with those who are closely associated with topics under investigation that are considered 'sensitive'.

Sensitive research

We defined our research as 'sensitive'. Our own previous research experience has taught us that respondents can often feel uncomfortable when discussing issues to do with 'race', diversity and social inclusion, particularly when these issues are related to respondents' own experiences in the classroom. Sensitive research is defined as occurring '... if it requires disclosure of behaviours or attitudes which would normally be kept private or personal, which might result in offence or lead to social censure or disapproval, and/or which might cause the respondent discomfort to express' (Wellings et al., 2000, p. 256). In addition, Robertson (2000) argues that sensitive research may include research that involves the private sphere of individuals – for instance, experiences that respondents may not have previously voiced or thought about. Others have argued that sensitive research encompasses '... studies in which there are potential consequences or implications, either directly for the participants in the research or for the class of individuals represented by the research' (Sieber & Stanley, 1988, p. 49).

Even though all research has implications and consequences, some research may be sensitive for particular vulnerable groups to engage in. Research that questions issues of racism and exclusion will challenge respondents to think about their own positions and identities as teachers in the classroom. Such issues will also enable respondents to review their own opinions. For these reasons, qualitative, in-depth interviews were used to enable respondents to open up and talk freely about their own experiences in the classroom and how their identities are affected by these experiences. Qualitative interviews enabled respondents to speak about issues in their own words and from their own experiences (Campbell, 2002). In-depth interviews were used with respondents as they provided the best means of enabling respondents to speak about their views on 'race' and racism and the teaching of these subjects, as such interviews

'. . . seek to build the kind of intimacy that is common for mutual self-disclosure' (Johnson, 2002, p. 103).

Feminist research

As Feminists our aim was to conduct the research in ways consistent with the basic principles of Feminist research. We wanted to be reflexive about the research process – that is, to stand back and examine the research process itself, '. . . to explore the process of research in more depth, to locate all facets of researchers' identities – values, beliefs and emotions – within the research context' (Campbell & Wasco, 2000, p. 788). In particular, the research was carried out from a Feminist perspective as it paid specific attention to the notion of differences and issues of power in the research relationship. As Hesse-Biber and Leckenby (2004) state, the Feminist approach to methodology '. . . allows for new types of questions about women's lives and those of other/ed marginalized groups to be addressed within their respective fields of research' (p. 210). In this research about 'race', it was important to build rapport with the respondents. As Fontana and Frey (2005) state:

> . . . it is paramount to establish rapport with respondents; that is, the researcher must be able to take the role of the respondents and attempt to see the situation from their viewpoint rather than superimpose his or her world of academia and preconceptions on them. (p. 708)

At the same time, Black Feminist researchers have argued that Feminist methods have actually excluded and further marginalized the position of non-White women and researchers (Hill-Collins, 1991; Phoenix, 1987). Consequently there is growing literature which explores the experiences of minority ethnic researchers (Bhavnani, 1993; Bhopal, 2009; Maylor, 2008; Mirza, 2009).

'Race', class and gender

As was noted above, a total of 30 interviews were conducted with students in 2 universities. Of these, all ten of the interviews in the first university, and a further ten in the second university, were conducted by a researcher (Andy[3]). The remaining ten in the second university were conducted by the first-named author of this book. Andy is a White, middle-class, 35-year-old male researcher. He has some experience of conducting interviews. We were particularly interested to examine whether the identity of the researcher would impact on the respondents, in terms of how open they might be about speaking about 'race', how they viewed the questions and in turn how they viewed the researcher. The majority of the respondents were White and from middle-class backgrounds, only a minority were from working-class backgrounds and only four were from minority ethnic backgrounds (one of whom was an international student from France).

In his feedback, Andy stated that he did not feel uncomfortable asking respondents questions to do with 'race', racism, identity, social justice and inclusion. He also stated that the respondents themselves did not feel threatened by him, and neither did they feel uncomfortable being asked about such issues. Instead, he found it quite easy to establish a rapport with the respondents so that they felt relaxed and confident when answering his questions.

By contrast, in the interviews that I (the first-named author of this book) conducted, there were several occasions when I felt that the respondents were uncomfortable speaking about issues to do with 'race', and particularly about their own experiences of racism. Some felt afraid to say things, for fear of hurting my feelings or upsetting me:

> I feel quite bad saying this to you. I hope you don't mind but there are members of my family who you might think were racist because of some of the things they say, but I don't think they really are.

> I feel quite ashamed when I sit here and tell you that I have seen some people who I know – not my friends – say racist things about other people and I have not challenged them about it or told them that they're wrong.

Furthermore, some of the respondents used my identity as an Asian woman in comparison to their own as teachers, particularly when discussing the teaching of 'race' and diversity:

> You see, I think pupils would react differently to how race is taught by different people. If it was someone like you, say, then they might take you more seriously because you are Asian and you probably know more about these issues than say me because I am White and have not had those experiences.

Another respondent articulately stated this position as follows:

> I don't think that race should be just taught by say Black people or Asian people, because that would just put it in a box and you say you have to be an ethnic minority to understand issues to do with race. But it shouldn't be like that. If you are a good teacher then you should be able to teach about anything regardless of your background or your ethnicity.

Other respondents spoke about class:

> Even though you and I are different . . . from different class backgrounds, say, we know we can communicate with each other, and that is what you have to be able to do in the classroom no matter what it is you're teaching, whether it's about race or about the weather.

Some respondents appeared to want to make sure that they said the 'right thing' and tell me the 'correct answers':

> I want to make sure I can answer your questions properly and tell you the right answers for your project because I think it is important that we all think about issues to do with race and how that impacts in the classroom for us as teachers.

Research has shown that our gender, 'race' and class can have a significant impact on the research relationship and the research process itself (Bhopal, 2010; Liamputtong, 2007). Some researchers have argued that this should be seen simply as part of the process of conducting research (Letherby, 2003). It seemed that those respondents who spoke to Andy did not feel uncomfortable speaking with him about issues to do with 'race' and racism. They did not necessarily feel that they would upset him with their responses. Song and Parker (1985) have argued being an outsider (from a different ethnic group from that of the participants) can actually encourage respondents to be more open about their experiences. Similarly, Reay (1996) has written about the difficulties of being too close to the respondents (of the same class background) and the effect that this can have on the research process and the collection of data.

In conducting our research we considered the identity of the researcher in the research process and the effect that our own identities would have on the research process. Some researchers have argued that 'ethnic matching' of the interviewer and the respondent, and the impact that researcher identity has on the data collected, should be considered at all stages of the research relationship (Bhopal, 2010). Gunaratnam (2003) states:

> At one end of this spectrum is the choice to subsume the complexities of subjectivity and social positioning under over-arching categories (be they racial, ethnic, cultural religious and/or linguistic); at the other end is the choice to recognize and work through the complexities and contingency of multiple and cross-cutting subjective, biographical and social differences. (p. 82)

Of course the choice lies with the researchers themselves, Papadopoulos and Lees (2002), for example, state that ethnic matching is crucial in conducting all types of research and it is important for the research process to 'match' respondents with researchers as this encourages more sensitive research and '. . . encourages a more equal context for interviewing which allows more sensitive and accurate information to be collected. A researcher with the same ethnic background as the participant will possess "a rich fore understanding"' (Ashworth, 1986, p. 261). Other researchers have argued that, in relation to ethnicity, when matching strategies are used, 'race' is used as 'methodological capital' that is used to build rapport and trust and gain access to non-White communities (Gallagher, 2000).

On the other hand, Phoenix (2001) reminds us that ethnic matching can be exploitative of minority ethnic communities when participants may feel that the non-White interviewer has some control over the research, when in fact they do not. It is important, however, to strike a balance – for example, when researchers do not consider the effects of 'race', class and gender on the research relationship and this can lead to misunderstandings and misinterpretations in the research process and the data (Riessman, 1987). As Gunaratnam (2003) states:

> . . . interactions and methodological discourses, such as those relating to matching, are constructed in ways that spotlight the determining effects of one (homogenous) category of difference over another. This can serve to produce and re-produce the apparent dominance – and also manageability – of one category, simultaneously obscuring other forms of difference and power relations. (p. 85)

We have to be careful when considering whether 'ethnic matching' works in the research process and think about the wider implications that it can have. There are risks associated with 'ethnic matching' and we need to question how far the matching should go. Should we also match for gender, age and class, for example? Indeed, 'Matching poses its own, very thorny political and methodological questions that can unsettle assumptions about relations of commonality and difference' (Gunaratnam, 2003, p. 103).

When researching about 'race' and ethnicity, Knowles (1999) has argued that it is important for researchers to examine and analyse how 'race' works through narratives in the research, specifically through understandings of identity in respondents' narratives. Knowles uses a particular analytical approach to explore how identities are played out in the research process. She states that 'performed identities interact with research processes and have multiple possibilities' (p. 112). According to Knowles (2003), to understand society is to understand 'race', because it is central to our lives and to the ways in which society functions: 'If we want to understand race then we need an analytic framework that addresses divergent levels of scope and scale, for race is simultaneously very personal and built into the structures of societies and the global order of things' (p. 11).

Power differentials

Power is a concept that always exists in the research process, no matter what (Bhopal, 2009). Power relations are complex and sometimes the power lies with respondents and at other times with the researcher. Power shifts and changes during the research process; it is dynamic and constantly changing. There is generally the assumption that the balance of power lies with the researcher and not the respondent. However, this is not always the case as sometimes respondents can hold the power by withholding information or manipulating the research relationship. Researchers, on the other hand, can also have power in the research relationship; they can also manipulate the respondents and discard them once they have finished their research (see Reinharz, 1986). According to Giddens (1985), power exists in all types of research relationships and can be exerted by the researcher and/or the respondent and, because the researcher holds the power ostensibly by controlling all aspects of the research relationship, it is highly that unlikely an equal relationship will exist between the researcher and the respondent (Letherby, 2003). Moreover, Millen (1997) argues that as researchers we must be careful in the research relationship; we may be thinking that we are giving respondents (particularly women) the tools to be able to understand their lives, but in fact we may actually be disempowering them.

At the same time, the research relationship is constantly changing and is fluid; researchers may not always hold the balance of power as much as they think that they do (Cotterill, 1992). Furthermore, respondents may not necessarily feel that they need to be empowered by researchers or to be engaged in the production of knowledge for the purposes of research. From another perspective Paradis (2000) has argued that research does have the direct potential to be exploitative and suggests that '. . . research resembles a colonial economy when researchers enter the world of participants uninvited, extract a resource called data, process this resource into a product called theory, and use the product only toward their own ends' (p. 840). Certainly it is important for researchers to be aware of the effect that they have on respondents' lives and the influence of their knowledge and their lived experience on the research relationship (Lee, 2002). Of course the dangers involved in the research relationship around the unequal power balance between the researcher and the respondent can result in unintended disclosure in which respondents may reveal personal details of their lives as they may feel obligated to respond to interview questions that they may not otherwise have answered (Daly, 1992).

Research in Australia

Researcher identities

A principal theme of this book is that the character and impact of identity and pedagogy as enacted in higher education systems are heavily influenced by the social and political contexts in which those systems are situated – in this case, in the UK and Australia. Correspondingly a major premise of this chapter is that researching racialized identities is also significantly affected by those contexts and also by the identities, experiences and aspirations of the researchers.

Indeed, we see one of the strengths of the book as being the fact that, despite several crucial commonalities of purpose and perspective, the two authors exhibit very different identities and sets of experiences. The position of the first-named author (Kalwant Bhopal) was addressed in the previous section of the chapter; now the situation of the second-named author (Patrick Alan Danaher) is outlined and located against the backdrop of salient ethical and political issues in broader Australian research into racialized identities.

Like contemporary many Australian citizens, I (Patrick) am a White Australian with English heritage on my mother's side and Irish heritage on my father's side. I was born in Pretoria, South Africa, to where my mother and her parents had emigrated from England after World War II, but my parents and I moved to Australia (where my father had been born) when I was 3 months old, and so my conscious memory of South Africa is from the post-apartheid era, when my mother, one of my brothers and I attended a conference in Johannesburg and did some limited travelling in the country in 2001. (These autobiographical elements are more fully developed in Coombes, Danaher, & Danaher, forthcoming.)

Like Kalwant in the UK, I have conducted a number of research projects related to minority ethnic groups and their identities in Australia. Some members of the Australian fairground or show communities (Danaher, 2001) and circus communities (Danaher, Moriarty, & Danaher, 2009) have belonged to such groups. (Similarly, minority ethnic identities have been a significant theme in research that I conducted with members of Traveller Education Support Services in England [Danaher, Coombes, & Kiddle, 2007].) Likewise an oral history (Danaher, 1991) of 'The Coming of the Light', the arrival of the London Missionary Society in the Torres Strait Islands, located between Queensland's northern coast and Papua New Guinea, entailed conducting several interviews with Islanders on Thursday Island and Darnley Island in the Strait. Other co-authored research has included evaluating three Aboriginal and Torres Strait Islander access certificate programmes at the Rockhampton College of Technical and Further Education (Danaher & Danaher, 1993–4), exploring the impact of competition on teacher education at an Australian university (including student identity issues) (Danaher, Gale, & Erben, 2000) and examining the effectiveness of a specialist distance education in-service programme for Torres Strait Islander teachers working in the Torres Strait (Lamb, Arizmendi, Stewart-Dore, & Danaher, 2002). I have also co-edited research publications, and have helped to facilitate the bringing together of the associated research findings, related to disrupting binaries that marginalize minority groups in various ways (Midgley, Tyler, Danaher, & Mander, 2011), the professional identities of educators working with variously marginalized learners (Anteliz, Coombes, & Danaher, 2010) and the capacity or otherwise of open and distance learning approaches to teacher education to enhance the school-level educational outcomes of variously marginalized pupils (Danaher & Umar, 2010).

In engaging in these several research projects that have involved to varying degrees studying the identities – including in many cases the racialized identities – of members of minority communities, I have been conscious that my status as a White Australian male and as a member of the academy has strongly influenced who I am and how I approach the complex processes of research design and data collection and analysis. Furthermore, I have acknowledged the possible risks associated with members of the mainstream society conducting research with representatives of minority groups, whether racialized or otherwise. For instance, I have commented (Danaher, 1998) on three different but equally potentially deleterious categories of interaction between majority researchers and minority respondents: presuming to advocate on behalf of the minority group; appropriation of the group's difference and otherness; and complicity in helping to perpetuate the group's marginalization. It is clearly crucial to move beyond these categories of researcher–respondent interaction to other and more enabling forms of contact.

Researching identities

Some of those more productive and transformative kinds of interactions between researchers and participants have been identified in the Australian literature about conducting research with racialized minorities. For example, a relatively recent theme in this literature has been the acknowledgement of the existence of distinctive Indigenous ways of knowing and of the need to respect those knowledge systems and to understand their influence on how Indigenous Australians might participate in specific research projects (Brown, 2010; Harvey, 2009; Kitson & Bowes, 2010; Nelson, 2009). The values underpinning this acknowledgement have been encapsulated as '. . . reciprocity; respect; equality; responsibility; survival and protection; and spirit and integrity' (Knight, Comino, Harris, & Jackson-Pulver, 2009, p. 467).

Similar strategies have been demonstrated as being effective in conducting research with other minority ethnic communities in Australia. For example, Vakalahi and Ihara (2011) state that their research with Tongan grandparents living in Australia required them to enact their roles and responsibilities as integral members of the community with whom they were researching, rather than remaining separate from and independent of that community:

> . . . the skills and cultural sensitivity of the research team are essential to the completion of a study. In this case, the inclusion of [Tongan] grandparents in the team showed respect for the existing power structure in the culture. . . . [M]embers of the research team embraced a role of service to their community and easily accepted direction from and responded to the needs of their community. The team consistently engaged in ongoing communication, consultation, and negotiation with members of the community, which informed their continuous development of competencies and also led to mutual understanding and informed consent . . . (p. 234)

Likewise, in articulating particular strategies used to design and carry out research with newly arrived refugee youths in Australia, Block, Warr, Gibbs and Riggs (2012/in press) contend unequivocally that:

> . . . promoting ethical practice and methodological validity are mutually reinforcing objectives and illustrate how processes of ethical reflexivity were applied to resolve methodological challenges, promote [the] autonomy and capacity of research participants and enhance the potential for outcomes to be rigorous and useful.

All of this reinforces that, like the fundamental issue of identities and pedagogies in higher education for minority groups in the UK and Australia with which this book is concerned, conducting research about that issue is complex, contested and sometimes controversial. Also like the issue that it is researching, the research is subject to the impact of broader social and political forces and to the influence of the character of the higher education systems in the two countries. In many ways, just as minority ethnic community members striving to access and engage in higher education often need bigger reserves of determination and resilience than their majority counterparts, so too researching in this field is not for the faint-hearted. Certainly these researchers need to develop strategies that are faithful to the participants and that are also true to the researchers' ethics and worldviews.

This chapter has elaborated some of the issues and dilemmas attendant on collecting and analysing the empirical data presented in the next chapter, as well as involved in conducting research about racialized identities more broadly. We turn now to present a theoretically informed synthesis of those empirical data.

Notes

1   Multiverse is a website funded by the TDA for teacher educators and student teachers to address the needs of minority ethnic pupils. It provides resources for student teachers to use in the classroom to address issues of racism, inclusion and educational underachievement.

2   The GCSE is an academic qualification awarded in a specific subject usually taken at the age of 16 in England.

3   This is a pseudonym.

6

Student Understandings of
Racialized Identities

This chapter concentrates specifically on the findings of comparative empirical research in relation to student and tutor perspectives and understandings of racialized identities in the UK and Australia. The chapter also explores the discourses by which students understand what it means to be White and what it means to be Black from the perspectives of local/domestic and international students. The research draws upon rich, qualitative, in-depth data to examine the different facets and themes of identity and pedagogy within the context of belonging and exclusion within higher education.

Research in the UK

The data for this section of the chapter are based on interviews conducted with a total of 30 students who were training to become teachers on primary and secondary PGCE courses at one traditional university in the South East of England. As discussed in the previous chapter, a total of 104 students participated in questionnaire surveys from which we were able to ascertain views of varying degrees of specificity on 'race', diversity and inclusion. We also conducted interviews with a total of 15 tutors, 5 from the university where the students completed the surveys, and 10 from another university with a similar intake of students and staff in relation to the demographics and ethnic make-up of those students and staff. The tutors in both institutions were all teaching on the primary or secondary PGCE courses. All had been involved in this teaching for a minimum of at least five years. This chapter focuses on the findings from the in-depth qualitative interviews conducted with the students; it also provides a case-study example of one tutor. (The results of the questionnaire surveys and the interviews with the other tutors are being reported in other publications.)

The majority of students who agreed to be interviewed were from White backgrounds and only a small minority were from non-White minority ethnic backgrounds. Out of the 30 students who participated in the interviews, only 3 were from African-Caribbean backgrounds (one of whom was an international student from France), 2 from Asian Indian backgrounds and 2 were mixed race (White British and African, White British and Indian). The majority of tutors who participated in the interviews were from White British backgrounds; only four were from minority ethnic backgrounds (including one from an African-Caribbean background, one from a British Indian background and one from a Turkish background).

Student perspectives: Understanding the terms

'Race'

All of the respondents were asked how they understood concepts such as 'race', diversity and inclusion. The majority understood the concept of 'race' in relation to identity and where they came from, specifically their cultural backgrounds. The term 'race' was used synonymously by many of the participants with the term 'ethnicity'. It was used as a descriptor to define the 'races' and cultural backgrounds to which individuals belonged to. Julie,[1] a primary PGCE student, said:

> Well, to be honest when you mention the term 'race', it's a bit like talking about ethnicity. It's really a way of categorizing people; that's what I would say and I think that's how we are led to understand the term. These days you wouldn't use the term 'race', would you? You would just say, 'Which ethnic group is that person from?' I think 'race' is a bit old fashioned and some people may see it as being a bit 'old hat' and not that pc [politically correct], so it's better to use the word 'ethnicity' because it kind of means the same thing, doesn't it?

Peter, on the other hand, was more cynical and felt that 'race' as a concept was used as a way of compiling statistics for government use:

> The word 'race' is used really to get statistics on things. It's a way of putting people into boxes and categorizing them and saying they're this 'race' and they're that 'race'. It's used for research purposes in order to generate statistics,

but sometimes it can be used wrongly and used to say what the government want to say about certain groups. So you have to be careful but, if you want to find out who is doing what, a lot of the time you need to know who those people are and where they come from. I suppose it's sort of a way so that you can understand the workings of society.

Diversity

When asked about the concept of diversity, the majority of respondents spoke about *difference* in relation to the recognition that in the classroom pupils are from differing backgrounds and this has to be taken on board and seen in a positive light. Many of the participants felt that it was important for teachers to be honest about diversity rather than using it as a 'tick box' exercise and thinking about it for the sake of being inclusive. Andrew, who described himself as 'Black British' said:

> I think all these terms like 'race' and 'diversity' are just buzzwords at the moment and what they do is demonstrate that we *have to* think about difference and the implication that has for teaching in the classroom [original emphasis]. If we didn't recognize that diversity existed then how could we teach? We have to be sensitive to different people and their needs. We can't just do it because we're told to do it; we have to believe in what we're doing. It can't just be an exercise we do because we have met some objective for the school.

At the same time as recognizing that diversity and difference were important and had to be taken on board and acknowledged in the classroom, Andrew was particularly cynical about the terms:

> Oh, it all seems very popular at the moment, all these words. Everything is focused on how diverse you are, how you include every person, every different person. I used to work in the legal courts in [name of city] and they were very focused on diversity, or *appeared* to be [original emphasis]. They had lots of courses on how to be diverse, how to treat people equally. I think it's very popular at the moment not to discriminate and to be seen to be diverse. But when you looked at the legal courts all the lawyers were White and there were some Black lawyers but more Asian, but I would say it was more White people who were in the positions of power. And that exists everywhere, even in teaching. On the one hand there is the emphasis on diversity, but on the other hand you just look at the workforce and all the people in the top positions happen to be White.

Although he was aware of the importance of diversity and its impact on society and the professions, Andrew drew on competing discourses in his analysis of the situation. On the one hand, he recognized that is important to be diverse or inclusive but at the same time he argued that it made no real difference to the diversity of the workforce, as those in powerful positions tended to be from White backgrounds. Sean, on the other hand, who was from a traditional, middle-class background, felt that the importance of diversity was crucial in the school setting and something that all schools and teachers should strive for. However, he recognized that sometimes it was a difficult goal to achieve:

> Diversity to me is something that is always there and whenever you are faced with a class of children you have to think about it, just like you have to think about it when faced with a lecture hall of trainee teachers like us. You will always have a diverse range of backgrounds of people in one class and you have to address that; you can't simply ignore it. And in many ways even a fairly homogenous class can be quite diverse; you need to know the backgrounds of your pupils. They could all be White, but some of them might come from very poor backgrounds and others could be very upper class. Their backgrounds will always affect how they look at things and as teachers we really have to think about diversity and bring it into the classroom at all times, even if at first glance it might not seem so obvious. I think the whole thing around diversity and inclusion is very difficult to achieve, but that doesn't mean we can't try. We have to try and give every individual kid an opportunity, a chance; otherwise you could fail as a teacher.

Marian, an international student from France, understood diversity to mean differences related to personal histories and experiences and she related these to religion. She herself was from a Muslim background and religion was an important part of her life. She was the only student on the course who wore a headscarf and identified herself as a Muslim:

> Diversity is an interesting concept to me and in our country [France] it means more about your own personal history and where you come from. We have had lots of controversies about our religion [Islam] and the wearing of the headscarf so to me diversity is recognition of your personal history – whatever history that is – it could be related to your religion or it could be related to the personal experiences that you have. And as teachers we will bring our own personal experiences into the classroom; we cannot help that. To me diversity is about where you come from and your experiences and history and for me that is all focused on my religion because it is such a big

part of my life. It is my life really because everything I do is based on the principles of Islam. I have to take my religion into the classroom because you can see from looking at me that I am a Muslim woman and I think that could be a positive thing because it could help children see Islam in a positive way.

Marian went on to discuss the impact of the 'war on terror' and the effect that it had had on her life in France and in the UK. She was adamant that becoming a teacher would help to break down stereotypes of Muslims being seen as terrorists and religious fanatics:

You know that since 9/11 [terrorist attacks on the World Trade Centre and the Pentagon in the USA on 11 September 2001] there have been lots of attacks on Muslims in France and I know there have been lots of things going on here [in the UK] since 7/7 [suicide bombings in London on 7 July 2005]. But as a Muslim woman going into a school – and when it is obvious that I am a Muslim – that can help the pupils think about Muslims differently and know that we are not all the way the media and TV wants to depict us. So if you can use diversity to stop people thinking about certain things in certain ways then that has to be a good thing for the pupils and the whole school.

Inclusion

When discussing the concept of inclusion, many of the students felt that inclusion was a hazy and unclear concept and some students did not make any distinction between 'inclusion' and 'diversity', but saw both terms as being part of the same thing. Many students defined the concept in relation to *exclusion*. Janet, a mature-aged student, was aware that inclusion was important in her teaching course and defined it as follows:

I would define it the opposite way. I would say that it's making sure that no one is *excluded*, because for me inclusion is something that should be happening all the time anyway, regardless of what is going on in the classroom [original emphasis]. It shouldn't be something that you have to think about and say, 'Okay, today I'm going to include all of the kids that I teach'. It should be an automatic thing. It's a very important facet of teaching that people should know about. It's difficult for me to think about it too much because I come from the opinion that it's something that you should be doing anyway and it should be an automatic thing and anything that you're doing different is wrong.

Sam, on the other hand, was very aware of issues of inclusion as he was interested in teaching about inclusion through the History curriculum. He made a conscious effort to make sure that he was inclusive in all of his lessons and wanted all students and tutors to take inclusion seriously:

> I don't really know how to define inclusion and to be honest I don't know how best to be inclusive. But in my subject – History – we have to try and think about how to include people from minority backgrounds without resorting to tokenism. One of the questions that I grapple with all the time is – should I talk about the influence of slavery here in the UK and, if I do, how would that make the Black students in my class feel? Or if I talk about Colonialism and Imperialism, how would that make some of the Asian students feel? Would it make them feel that they are being included and we care about what History has done to them or would it make them stand out and feel embarrassed or ashamed? These are things that you have to think about, because you want to be inclusive, but how do you do it without it appearing to be tokenistic or even patronizing? That's what's hard about inclusion, I think – striking the right kind of balance.

Sam also felt that inclusion was a double-edged sword. He questioned whether being inclusive meant that you were actually being *exclusive* (as discussed above). Sam was training in a predominantly White, middle class, secondary school in a middle-class, affluent area. He was worried about how inclusion would be received in such an environment:

> When you talk about inclusion to a mixture of people – say from all different ethnic groups and all different backgrounds – it sort of makes it much easier because they know that it is important and see it as something that is quite normal. But, like I said, it's hard to know how best to be inclusive. In one of the classes at the moment, there's this Black boy who has come from quite a rough area in [name of city] where he was involved in gangs and knives. And from what I've observed he's been allowed to get away with all sorts – more so than the other boys in the class. I think, because their teachers have a fear of appearing racist or even of singling him out, they let him get away with things. Also, because the school is predominantly White, they are trying to be too careful. They have to treat him like the others – if he does something wrong he should be told off – just like the other kids.

Sam was very thoughtful and reflective about his own classroom practice and concluded: 'It's really interesting to watch the teachers and how they treat the minority kids, and that's inclusion – it's a tricky thing.'

Joanne, on the other hand, expressed her concerns about inclusion in relation to how 'good practice' worked in schools. She too was passionate about inclusion, but was unsure how it actually *worked* in practice, and particularly emphasized the importance of inclusion in terms not just of education but also of thinking about the contributions of all communities. She took a holistic view of inclusion and thought about it in terms of the whole of society rather than just the institution of the school:

> To me, inclusion is a difficult one because I like to think that we all do it in our everyday lives, but I think that would be too optimistic wouldn't it? To me, it has to be about what is happening in the classroom and how inclusion works out in practice; it's about how it translates in the classroom. And that would be related to how you do certain things and how you approach different students in your class. But this has to be taken outside of the classroom as well. It has to be a thing you think about all the time in your everyday life – it has to be about inclusion in the community as well, not just in an educational sense. If you don't have it in an educational sense, how can you have it in the community sense? It's about putting it into practice. You have to take it from the classroom into the rest of society; that's the only way that inclusion can work. Otherwise you could say that the classroom is an artificial environment because you could be inclusive in the classroom but not think about inclusion in the community and in society. It has to work in all spheres of life, not just in education terms.

At the same time as being optimistic about inclusion, Joanne was also rather pessimistic and in reality did not really think that inclusion was a goal that teachers could reach:

> Ummm – I think it's [inclusion] perhaps not working as well as it should be in schools. Not just about 'race', but also about language as well. I was at a school which was in a poor area and there was a big population of EAL [English as an Additional Language] students and there wasn't the support that they needed so they were getting behind in all the subjects. There wasn't anything that would include them in the lessons. And to me *that is not inclusion*; in fact, those kids are being failed by the system and will not do well when they leave. That is *exclusion* [original emphasis].

Joanne saw the need to implement 'good practice' in schools, yet wasn't sure how this would or should happen in practice. She did not feel that the notion of inclusion should be based on separating or singling students out as different; she felt that this would in fact defeat the whole object of the goals of inclusion:

I think a lot of work needs to be done sort of – sort of looking at inclusion, say, in preparation for allowing those students [with EAL] and students who have other needs before they can participate into the mainstream classrooms. And I don't think the support is there at the moment, so that makes me want to question whether inclusion is something that actually exists in practice, in the classroom, or is it just there in the policies, sort of like a tick box exercise? What's the point of having these policies on inclusion if we can't provide those children with the language support that they need? What's the point of those children not being in mainstream classrooms because they can't cope? There are a lot of issues that we need to think about in relation to inclusion. But they are big issues and can sometimes conflict with the day to day running of the school. But we have to try and think of ways that we don't fail those kids who can't speak English; we have to try and be inclusive.

Similarly, Jamie felt that inclusion was something that students were made to think about from a theoretical perspective, but was not convinced whether inclusion was really happening in the classroom:

To me to be inclusive you have to do certain things in the classroom. Inclusion is about doing stuff; you may need to talk about it, to theorize it, to understand it. But at the end of the day, it's about *what you do* in the classroom [original emphasis]. To me, I have to think about what I have done in the classroom so that every child in that classroom feels they can benefit from what I have taught and none of those kids feel[s] like they have been left out. Sometimes that can be a hard thing to do and I feel that as trainee teachers *we should be taught* how we can do this on a practical basis rather than just the theory of doing it [original emphasis].

One of the ways that Jamie thought about inclusion was through his teaching of History. Like Sam above, he was keen to teach students about the diversity of British history through the inclusion of events that were rarely discussed:

Inclusion is a key focus of our course because you can teach about it in different ways; you just have to be a bit imaginative. In history, for example, the one chance I really had to get the students to think about inclusion was about talking about the representation of Gypsy groups in the holocaust and also the contribution of ethnic minority troops in the British Empire to the war effort, which are things that a lot of kids and a lot of adults aren't aware of. So that means that the other pupils also learn about these things and might go home and tell their parents about it. It surprises many of the pupils because they have often said that they didn't know that Gypsies were persecuted in the holocaust and they didn't know that lots of ethnic minorities have contributed to not just the war effort but now in Afghanistan. This can sort to help break down stereotypes and prejudices that they and even their families might have about these groups.

Jamie was passionate about history and was keen to stress that History was a subject that could deal with inclusion in different ways and for him it was something that he did not have to think about:

To me, it comes naturally really. Even before I decided I wanted to become a teacher, I would say I was inclusive. I come from a very liberal background where both my parents are very into things like equal rights for everyone, so it could be that. We had a discussion the other day with some of the students about the origins of maths and algebra and as we know it first originated from the Islamic world and some of the kids thought that was just rubbish because they didn't know about it. But that's how you can use your knowledge as a teacher to break down those stereotypes; that's what teaching should be about. Of course it's about getting the kids to think and learn about History but it's also about challenging their stereotypes and making them think about things in a different way.

Rebecca, on the other hand spoke about inclusion as being a goal that could never be achieved. She spoke about inclusion in relation to gender:

I'm not sure that you can really have inclusion. For example, if you had a class of equal boys and girls, does that mean there is inclusion and they all get treated equally in the same way? It doesn't, because if you think about it boys are more competitive and forthright and would want to answer questions more than the girls and they may want to prove something. So does that mean that you respond more to the boys than you do to the girls? It [inclusion] is something that is hard to achieve and I don't think you can have inclusion in the classroom. The way that boys and girls are treated at schools just gets translated into the wider world of work and that's why you don't have inclusion in the workforce or in other places.

White and Black identities

When they were asked about how they would define themselves and about their own identities, the majority of students defined themselves in terms of their ethnic identities rather their visual identities, based on colour. In fact, many of the respondents felt that such notions of identity (White and Black) were crude and did not represent their cultures, histories or backgrounds. Many of them stated that such definitions of being White or Black did not mean or say anything about their identities when used on their own; rather the terms had meaning only if they were associated with their ethnic and cultural backgrounds. When students spoke about White identities, they spoke about them in relation to being privileged, advantaged and in a position of power compared to those who were Black. Whiteness was considered the norm; it was an identity against which all other non-White identities were judged or on which they were based. It was seen as the starting point of how other identities were defined; it was the one identity that was considered acceptable and the norm not just in British society, but also in society worldwide. Whiteness carried a universal connotation of acceptance and privilege.

By contrast, respondents understood that the category or identity of being Black was seen in opposition to being White, as being disadvantageous and as an identity that would immediately exclude individuals based on what they looked like (although the respondents themselves stated that they did not have these views, but they asserted that most of society felt and thought this way). Only one student saw Black as being positive, powerful and something that had added 'cultural capital' and worth in relation to being fashionable and accepted and to having street credibility:

> I would say that a lot of the White kids are quite jealous of the Black kids, because being Black is associated with being cool [and] hip and as being very attractive. All the girls think that Black is cool, so I guess that most other kids want to be cool and accepted like the Black kids are.

When they were asked about their identities, many of the respondents distinguished between being British and being English. Jack was clear that his identity was British and *not* English:

> I would say that I'm British White and the reason why I say I'm British is because I actually have Scottish ancestry but I am very much – I see myself as English living, but obviously I wouldn't say I was English as I don't have that background at all.

When asked how people would define him, Jack immediately thought of his identity as being that of a White European:

> People would say that I'm English, but I mean really I'm a White British European, aren't I? I don't think anyone would define me as anything else.

But then you have to think that these things are just labels, aren't they? I don't really see what difference these things make, because we are all humans at the end of the day. I think we all make a great play of our backgrounds, but you have to look at it as though we're just all the same; we all have similar aspirations and we are striving for the same things.

Jack appeared to have a real sense of social justice; his view was that one's background and identity (being White and being Black) should not affect how we are seen in society. At the same time, he was aware of how differences affect people's lives:

I would like to think that people won't judge me because I am White and judge someone else because they are Black or Asian. That is what I think and believe and I hope that other people think that too. My girlfriend always tells me that I'm idealistic and think that everyone is good. That's one of the reasons I want to be a teacher, because I think you can see the good in everyone – no matter how bad other people may think they are. But I'm not naïve. I know that there are people out there who are prejudiced and who will say some outrageous things that could shock you. But I like to think that those people are in the minority and most people don't think like that.

At the same as being aware that everyone should be treated equally, Jack knew that his White identity was associated with advantages and privileges that Black people did not have:

I do hate to say this and I don't usually say things like this because I like to be positive and like to think that most people don't think this way – but in the UK, and in Europe even, it [being White] is still seen as an advantage – which is hard to believe in the 21st century. You still read newspaper reports where unfortunately ethnic minority people find it harder to get jobs and particularly Black people and that's very concerning and it saddens me that this is still going on. I have seen it myself. For example, I have observed people – Black people actually – being treated in an inferior way. People sometimes have a different, negative attitude in how they speak to them, and that bothers me. What gives them the right to do that? They don't know them or know anything about them.

Jack had experienced racism himself as an observer and explained how it always shocked him each time that he had experienced it:

I remember when I was working in [name of supermarket] and there was a Black lady working there and she had been working there a long time. And, of all the people working on the tills and actually in the supermarket, she was the only Black person there from an ethnic group and I would say that really no one spoke to her and I wonder if that was because she was Black. It was a very White area.

Other students defined the identity of being Black as one that existed around judgements, generalizations and negative perceptions based on the colour of one's skin:

Some people are very tolerant and my view is you should accept people for who they are and not make judgements about them based on what they look like – and that's not just [the] colour of their skin; it's also about what clothes they are wearing and how they speak. But, when I was at university, I remember there was somebody we had been working with for ages and he was into Samba music and he said, 'Just because I'm Black doesn't mean I know what Samba rhythms are'. And funnily enough I'd never actually seen him as Black before and he obviously was but it never occurred to me. It really shocked me, actually and I thought, 'how could I be thinking like that?'

But some of the students indicated that stereotypes could be positive as well as negative:

Some people have a negative perception of all non-White people full stop. that's because they are just racist and probably know nothing about the groups. But then you have the other perceptions – which are stereotypes as well – that all Asian people are very hard-working, successful and do well at school. But, if you break the Asian groups down, you see it's not all the Asian groups. It's the Indian, more middle-class ones who are doing well and not the others so much.

Penny was aware of the different stereotypes associated with being White, but she did not feel particularly proud of her Whiteness:

I wouldn't promote being White because of what it all stands for. It means you are in a position of privilege and of power and you will be treated in a certain way because you are White and you will be treated in a certain way because you are Black and that is quite frightening.

Andrew spoke about his identity of being White in relation to his gender: 'I am White, but for some people that would make me superior because I am White, because I am British and I suppose you could say because I am middle class and also male!' Andrew was aware that being White gave him an automatically privileged identity, particularly in the current climate:

> I think there is a lot of prejudice around at the moment about Asian people and their communities. People automatically think that all Asians are Muslims and so are terrorists and that really bugs me. It's just ignorance and people reading the *Daily Mail*.[2]

Andrew had thought a lot about his teaching and was very reflexive about how 'race' impacted in the classroom:

> Sadly, quite often the good schools are always in the middle-class, affluent areas. But I think it's important for all kids to know about different cultures, to break down the stereotypes and to think about what impact those stereotypes have. Unfortunately, it's the kids who are in the middle-class areas who seem to have the most stereotypes because they haven't come across anyone different in their lives.

Andrew also touched on the notion that Whiteness was seen by some people as giving them the right to think that they were superior:

> I think sometimes White people have this kind of attitude or understanding that makes them think this is *our* country and we have a right to be here and Black people don't [original emphasis]. I don't know, but I think they [White people] think that gives them some idea of authority like they have the right to define what it's worth [being Black]. It's like some White people think they are better than everyone else and that is just wrong.

Class and locality

Many of the respondents spoke about class and how this was related to 'race' and locality. For example, some respondents indicated that where people came from made a difference to how they were treated. Many of the respondents spoke about class in terms of how they and others were treated. Paul spoke about how he was treated because he had attended an independent, fee-paying school:

> I went to an independent school and I'm very conscious about that with some people; I would never reveal it to them. Which I know sounds bizarre, but there is definitely a feeling that if you go to an independent school you are posh and rich. And there is also the perception that, because you have money, you are a happy person. It's almost like the other way around; if you are poor then suddenly it's going to be a miserable experience. I have had

the mickey taken out of me because I went to an independent school. And when I tell people I can play the organ, they quite often say, 'Where did you learn that?', and you tell them it was at [name of school], and then they sort of change their opinion of you. So I do think there is some prejudice against your class if you went to an independent school.

Locality in relation to class background was also an issue that many of the students spoke about, particularly in relation to accent. Sarah was from a middle-class background and commented on how her accent was seen by both the pupils and other teaching staff at the school:

I used to work in a White school where, if a Black teacher came in, then it would be a talking point. Also I remember being in one school [where,] because my accent is a bit home counties or southern, it was really picked up and people thought I was posh! But then we also had someone from London who was in Brixton and Stockwell and his accent was seen as a cockney accent, when in fact it wasn't. I know the staff and the pupils do make judgments about me because of the way I speak. They think I am really posh but I'm not! This is just the way my family speak and the way we are.

Sarah was, however, aware that her accent would be seen by some as an advantage:

I do think that people would treat me in a certain way because of how I speak. That could mean they treat me in a better way compared to other people. But I don't think that should happen because it just reveals another sort of prejudice that exists in society.

Many of the respondents felt that class had a significant impact on how they and others were seen in the classroom and in some cases featured more strongly in responses than 'race' or ethnicity. Juliette said:

I think the type of school I went to was quite posh or middle class and I am from that kind of background so I kind of mix with people like that. I mix with posh Black people and posh Asian people as well. I don't think in the situations that I am in 'race' plays a very important part. It's more to do with your background, how you speak and the kind of school that you went to. I think it's more to do with your class and how you associate with that identity.

For Juliette, her class background played a significant role in her life, but entering the teaching profession had highlighted her class identity more so than she had expected that it would:

> I think we all make judgments about people based on how they speak and where they come from. But, when you go into teaching, you can't really do that unless you teach in a private school where most of the students are from similar backgrounds – but that's changing now anyway – but you have to be open to difference and you have to be tolerant, otherwise I don't think you could be a successful teacher. I didn't think my class would make a difference in terms of how I am seen, but it has and the pupils do make judgments about you and say that you are posh!

Juliette felt that teaching had the reputation of being a predominantly White, female, middle-class profession that did not attract students from diverse backgrounds:

> I do think that teaching is very White, female and middle class. Even in very diverse schools, like the one I was in before Christmas, it had a big mix of different students from so many backgrounds and I think there were more than 30 different languages spoken there, but all the teachers – and I mean all of them – were White. How can that happen? To me, it is a worry because we need to have more ethnic minorities in teaching so that they can be a role model to students and also they are more likely to understand some of the cultural issues going on with some families. Also for the pupils, if they see someone who they think will understand their own culture and experiences, they might approach them if they have any problems or worries.

Juliette went on to describe how in this particular placement the teaching staff did not necessarily engage or make an effort to include students from minority backgrounds:

> I don't think the teaching staff gave the students a sense of belonging like they could have. As a teacher, you need to be aware that students are from different backgrounds and you have to think about what you are teaching and how you impart that information to them. You also have to think about why they are there as well. It's not just a job; being a teacher is something you have to think about all the time, and you have to think about how you can achieve a sense of achievement for all students, no matter what their ethnic or class background is.

Teaching about 'race'

For many of the students, one of the reasons that they had gone into teaching was to make a difference to the students whom they were teaching and to be role models. In some cases, this was based on their having had negative experiences of their own teachers, who had actually discouraged them from doing well. For others, it was either because their parents were teachers or because they were passionate about their subject and wanted to share this passion with others.

From this perspective, Emily wanted to be a positive role model for pupils, despite (or because of) being aware that issues of racism were prevalent in classrooms:

> My teaching placement is quite challenging. The school I am in is in a very deprived area and there are lots of children who have certain views about ethnic minorities and that has to be challenged and the classroom is the best and safest place it can be challenged. I think as a teacher I have a great place as a role model. I mean, I do agree that we don't have enough ethnic diversity in education. I think you get some schools from the outside and they are very White [and] middle class, but you might not get that in the pupils. It might be difficult for the pupils and staff to get that connection that is necessary, so I think ethnicity is really important in the classroom.

Many of the students thought that racism existed in many schools and was a challenge for them. For Mary, this was one of the things that she wanted to change:

> Umm – actually I think in education we are very assuming that children understand and are fully aware of racial issues and I think we are pretty good at educating, but I would say actually sometimes we need to go back to basics. By that I mean that unfortunately there is still racial prejudice against Black people. I think people make a subconscious impression and perhaps treat them in different ways and that is clearly wrong. We have to be able to challenge those views and in our role as teachers we have to see that as part of our job. We shouldn't have to question it; we should just be able to do it without thinking about it and work from the premise that racism in any way is not acceptable in schools or in the classroom.

Dealing with racism in the classroom

Many of the students spoke about the training that they had received in their courses as being insufficient to deal with issues of 'race' and racism in the classroom. Although many did state that they had been taught about theories and policies of inclusion, 'race' appeared to be a side issue to this.

Jacky was acutely aware of this situation and felt that it was particularly important to her as she was from a mixed race background herself:

> We are told that there are ethnic groups and we have to be aware of inclusion in the classroom, but to be honest I don't think we are actually told that we may encounter racism ourselves if we're not White, or that racism still exists in the classroom and in schools. I think we are far too scared and shy at really investigating that. And, if you do encounter it, then because you're not told about it you don't expect it and also you don't know to deal with it. And that can be quite a scary thing when you're confronted by a classroom full of stroppy kids who have an opinion on everything!

Jacky was keen that pupils should discuss issues of racism publicly in the classroom, specifically so that the perpetrators of racism could understand the hurt and upset that they caused to others:

> I think it would be a good idea to get someone to talk about their experiences, if they could. If you had someone who had recently suffered what they perceive as either indirect or direct racial prejudice against them, if they talked about it, it could help them. Talking about it and talking about how they felt and what happened to them and how it offended them. I think we are very good at using all these strategies and policies, but we are not terribly good at asking people what they think and what has upset them, especially if they have had a bad experience of prejudice. I really do think that it needs to come from that end of the spectrum rather than the White, middle-class assumptions. That way, this can generate a better understanding from both sides.

Emily, as a White, middle-class woman, did not initially think that her background would affect her role as a teacher:

> I never considered my place as a White, middle-class woman in the classroom before I was made to think about it. Becoming a teacher, I never considered the impact my colour or my background would have. I mean in honesty, the only things I thought would have an impact would be the education that I have had and whether that is going to impact on the kinds of schools that want me because of their own prejudice. But I know now that some Black or Asian children may not be able to identify with me, but White, middle-class

pupils might. It has made me think about it and look at the classroom from a different perspective.

Penny, on the other hand, was also aware of her own class background in relation to her changing her position by entering the teaching profession, from being working class to becoming middle class:

> I think people might say things to me because of how I sound, the way I speak. It's more to do with the fact that they might think I am middle class, because I know I do sound middle class, which is quite strange, because I am really working class. I grew up on a council estate in a poor part of [name of city]; I don't know where I got this accent from! But that's quite interesting, isn't it? – the fact that you can sort of hide your class background but you can't hide your 'race'. Becoming a teacher has sort of made me middle class, but I still see myself as a working-class girl from a council estate. Some people might think that I'm at a disadvantage, but I think I'm at an advantage. I can use my working-class background to identify with working-class kids and let them know they can also go to university and have a profession, and that can only be a good thing.

Many of the respondents like Penny related notions of identity to visible markers of difference. Penny was aware that she could hide her working-class roots, but her Whiteness was far more difficult to hide, just as a Black person was unable to hide her or his non-White identity. Penny spoke about racism in contradictory ways. On the one hand, she was appalled that people used racist names to refer to those from minority backgrounds, but at the same time she defended them by not believing that they could be *really* racist, perhaps a view that she found difficult to comprehend and come to terms with:

> They [people whom she knows] make jokes about Black and Asian people, but they wouldn't go and bash people on the head because they thought they were from a different country or whatever. It's that inherent thing – let's make a joke about it, because it's okay to do that. Some of them even use racist names to make the jokes, but I don't really think they're racist because they're not members of the BNP [British National Party][3] and they wouldn't go around being aggressive to Black or Asian people.

Equally Penny stated that she would not tolerate name-calling or racism at any level in the classroom but that she would benefit from more training on how to handle racism in the classroom:

Apart from the fact that we've only had a lecture on it, I am still stuck with the same question I had to myself at the beginning, 'How do I treat that kid the same as the others and how do I not end up loading all these cultural attachments on him?' Inadvertently, I am obviously not going to do that. I think I am reasonably informed about these things, but I still think, 'How would I deal with racism and things like that?' I would never accept racist language from anyone in the classroom and would not expect anyone to be racist. But, if they were, then I would have to deal with it? I would find it a challenge really and would probably find it quite shocking.

Sheila was one of the few Black women in the course, and she was adamant that there was some recognition of 'race' and diversity in her teaching practice, but she also felt that there could be far more than what was currently on offer for students:

I do think that these days we are more on the ball. There's quite a lot of understanding of people's needs and their backgrounds and where they come from. Perhaps not necessarily with the PGCE – there should be more there for us, but, with the older teachers who have been around for a long time, I don't think there's that much understanding for them at all. Unless they are in a particularly diverse school, they won't come across those ['race' and diversity] issues at all. I guess they just bury their heads in the sand and don't investigate it; they just sort of deal with the students in front of them – those who are White. We should have specific training on 'race'. There isn't much at all and if you want to do it in any depth it's an optional subject. To me, it should be a compulsory topic so that everyone is aware of all the issues.

Omar, who was from a Turkish background, was passionate about teaching pupils from diverse backgrounds. For him, the greater diversity in the student population, the more exciting the teaching:

Why would you want to teach kids who were all from the same background – and by that I could mean their ethnicity, gender, religion, class or whatever? I love teaching kids from different Asian and Black backgrounds. At the school I'm in, there is a big population of Sikh children and also lots of Somali kids and that's great. They have a wealth of knowledge and information they can bring to the class that we can all learn from, me included. There's also a high population of kids from Eastern Europe and that's growing. As long as there is support for the communities, then it has to be a positive thing. But I'm not

so sure that those views are shared by the rest of the [teaching] profession
or the rest of society.

These student responses showed the complexities and different elements that
student teachers bring to their teacher training experiences. Their understandings
of identity were woven within their understandings of a diverse range of
differences such as their 'race', gender and class and also their own experiences
of learning in the classroom. What was clear were the different facets of identity
and how they translated into the classroom and how they were related to the
students' different roles as teachers and educators. They brought their own
identities into the classroom and were aware of the impact that these identities
might have had on pupils' learning.

Even more importantly, however, they were all aware how identities impact
on learning experiences. They all felt that inclusion and diversity were important
goals to be aimed for, but not all of them believed that they could be achieved.
Nevertheless, part of being a teacher for many of the respondents was the desire
to make a significant difference to the lives of pupils. Even if this were in small
steps, they felt that it would lead to greater and bigger differences, which could
impact positively on the school and the local communities. While racism was
recognized as something that continued to exist in society, the school was
constructed as an environment in which racist views and prejudiced could be
challenged. It was seen as a 'safe environment' in which these challenges could
take place. For some this was an uncomfortable experience, but for others it was
about 'making a difference'.

While the students had received some training on diversity, inclusion and
'race' (albeit in a theoretical fashion), all agreed that their institutions could
and should be doing more to equip students with greater skills to deal with
incidents of racism and prejudice as well as with a focused understanding of
these issues. This was particularly the case for those students who not only grew
up in predominantly White areas but also taught in mainly White schools. For
these students, issues of 'race' and diversity were more important, as teaching
about these issues helped to combat the stereotypes that pupils held about ethnic
minorities when they attended all-White schools.

What was clear from the data was the recognition that students were very
reflexive about their teaching practice and all of the students wanted to make a
difference in their teaching – some by being inclusive in their curriculum, others
by using engaging and innovative methods of teaching that would encourage
their own students to question racism and prejudice. The respondents were also
aware of the impact of their own identities on their teaching and how they could

use these identities in the classroom to engage and motivate students in their own learning experience.

Identities were also seen as shifting, changing and dynamic. Some of the students were reflexive about where they had grown up and how their own identities (such as their class position) had shifted once they had entered the teaching profession. What was clear, however, was that some identities were unable to be changed; those visible markers of difference, of being White and being Black, remained firmly part of their roles as teachers and educators.

We have presented in some depth the students' responses to the interview questions about racialized identities and their impact on pedagogy in higher education and the students' own learning and teaching experiences. We turn now to explore the case study of Mike, the pseudonym for one of the tutors who taught at one of the participating universities and who agreed to be interviewed for the research project.

Mike

Mike Smith was 42 years old and had worked in various secondary schools before leaving to take up a lectureship at one of the participating universities. He described himself as a White, middle-class male. Mike taught on the secondary PGCE programme and he also taught an optional module on Citizenship and Identity. Mike also taught history elements of the primary PGCE course.

Mike was a History graduate and History was his passion. Mike was particularly interested in how he could use History to teach about diversity and inclusion in the classroom. For Mike, inclusion was about making the curriculum accessible for all children. He particularly emphasized the importance of teachers within this role, which was to remove barriers to learning for some children and how teachers could work to make learning a more engaging and successful experience for the pupils. Mike recognized that inclusion was a difficult concept to define and to reach, but he was a firm believer in the notion that part (though not all) of inclusion was to do with making students *feel* welcome in a school with an ethos that they felt addressed the needs of *all* children.

For Mike, inclusion was not just about teaching particular subjects as part of the curriculum; it was much more than this. When Mike discussed inclusion, he particularly referred to physical needs and disabilities:

> I was fortunate in that the last school that I worked at, because we had a disabled unit in the school and so everything was specially set up for the kids and we had quite a big special needs department, so we were able to

take a whole range of children with a whole range of different needs and they were part of the mainstream schooling. I do think that sort of thing makes other children more accepting. That's what I think inclusion is about; it's about accepting all kinds of children with whatever disabilities they have. In our school it was physical disabilities; for others it could be other things. But inclusion can mean lots of different things to different people. It's about having that ethos in the school where you make *everyone* feel welcome whatever their backgrounds or disabilities [original emphasis].

Mike had thought a great deal about inclusion and he was very passionate about it, but he did not think that it was a reachable goal:

I don't think you can ever fully be 100% inclusive nor have 100% inclusive schools because I think by certain practices it just creates problems. Sometimes you might be able to include pupils, when in fact you may really be excluding them. That's the problem with a concept like inclusion. I don't know if there are schools that are completely inclusive. I'm sure many schools would say they were inclusive, but it must depend on how you deal with things on a day to day basis and then you have to stand back and say, 'Was that inclusive? Did it really work and who is it inclusive for?' It comes down to what you think education is for. It's not just to get kids through exams, and it's about a social aspect as well. They have to be prepared to go into the real world after they leave school. So inclusion has to be about all of those things. If you think you are being inclusive and kids leave school without knowing how to get on in the real world, and if you have not prepared them, can you say you have been inclusive?

Mike did not feel that the school curriculum was diverse. Instead he felt that there were different problems associated with the curriculum that contributed to the whole schooling experience being exclusive rather than inclusive (even though the aim was to be inclusive). Mike remarked on the ethnic make-up of the teaching profession which he said continued to recruit students from mainly White, female, middle-class backgrounds, despite the ethnic make-up of society and the move towards the *Every Child Matters Agenda*[4]:

I think diversity is something we should be doing to promote more effectively and it's something we don't do very well. We continue to recruit the same type of people we want to be teachers; we have to ask, 'Why is that? Why can't we break the mould and do something different?' We talk about the *Every Child Matters* Agenda all the time – and I teach about it – but we need to think about 'Who is that referring to? Does it really refer to people from *all* backgrounds [original emphasis]? We have to think about these things before we can get to the real crux of the issues. We need to think about the types of people we recruit to teach and the impact this has not only on the profession, but [also] on the pupils we are supposed to be including.

Mike felt that many teachers (particularly those who had been teaching for a long time) were too afraid to get out of their comfort zone, so that they continued to teach the same subjects day after day, without really thinking beyond their own (White, middle-class) experiences. As a White, middle-class male, Mike himself felt that his own identity had an impact on how he taught diversity. When teaching in predominantly White schools, Mike hadn't thought about diversity issues, but once he began training students to become teachers he thought about how he could use his own subject – History – to discuss diversity and inclusion.

Yet he did not feel confident as a White, middle-class male to discuss Black History. He was aware that his own identity as a White, middle-class male was one of privilege and advantage. However, in the last few years, his growing confidence had enabled him to become more assertive and to use History as a way of engaging students to discuss issues of 'race', racism and inclusion:

> I know there's lots of things about White privilege and actually there is a whole sense of things that are unspoken and I assume they just happen, so in a sense being White is a taken for granted position because you are White and you have those privileges. But I have become more confident in using my own subject of History to get the students to talk about how diversity and inclusion can work and how racism has affected how we view society. I think that it takes time as a White person to talk and teach about 'race' and racism, because the danger is that students – especially Black students – may think, 'What does he know about this subject? He's a White man'. So you have to be careful that you do it right and you don't exclude those students further and that you don't patronize them.

Being an historian, Mike felt that inclusion was an important issue, simply because the History that was traditionally taught in British schools was so White and British. Since teaching his own students, Mike hoped that he would have made some difference to how students thought about inclusion and more importantly how they could use their own subjects to be inclusive and to encourage their students to think about diversity, which they could then apply to the classroom experience. Mike also emphasized that it was important for students to understand that they could not let their own stereotypes influence how they perceived pupils, because doing so could lead to a categorization of different pupils based on their 'race', class and gender. Mike stated that sometimes students did this unconsciously, without realizing it:

> There is a tension that exists around inclusion and diversity. Because you have the perfect student who fits in and conforms and does everything, but then if they don't fit into that box you might treat them differently. And so I think there are some concerns there. You can teach trainees about Black underachievement and you know we need to do more to support that, but by actually labelling groups by saying, 'Black boys underachieve', you lose sight of the individual but at the same time you need to see who those individuals are. So I think there is a difficulty and a big tension there, and we have to know how to cope with that.

Mike also highlighted what he called 'the dangers of diversity', which in some cases did not give disadvantaged groups the opportunity to learn. He mentioned the effects of poverty and class and the impact that they had on learning:

> What about the poor kid who lives in a bed sit with his mum and has no dad? He can't afford pen and paper and comes to school wearing a torn uniform. His mum can't help him with the homework; she has to make sure her family are just surviving. What does that say about inclusion? You have to turn inclusion on its head. What sort of problems has that child got when he comes to school? Would you teach him the same way as you teach someone else or do you treat him differently because he is poor? Do you tell him off because he hasn't done his homework or do you tell off the rich kid who didn't do his homework because he couldn't be bothered?

Mike acknowledged that in reality teachers were not always aware of some of the issues that pupils had to cope with at home. But he did recognize that there were boundaries for some pupils that were affected by their own backgrounds and families. Mike felt that these boundaries were unfair:

> It seems grossly unfair to me that we have these boundaries in the classroom. In reality, it's not the same playing field for all the kids; some simply have an easier and better time than others. So what does that say about inclusion? That's what's wrong and I don't think teaching can really change that. We can try but I'm not sure if we can change it.

Mike had clearly thought a great deal about inclusion, diversity and issues to do with 'race' in the classroom. He was reflective about this experience; he was hopeful at the same times as being cynical. He knew that inclusion may be a goal that could never be reached, but he was determined to try. One of the ways that he wanted to try to change his own teaching was by using History as a means of understanding diversity and inclusion.

Research in Australia

The empirical research in Australia generally aligns closely with that in the UK reported in the previous section of the chapter, while allowing for differences derived from the varied cultural, political and systemic contexts in which trainee teachers and tutors enact their professional and personal identities. One discernible difference is that Australians are more likely to talk about 'ethnicity' than 'race' and about 'socioeconomic background' than 'class', although the underlying experiences are in many ways similar between the two countries. (More broadly, Armstrong, Armstrong and Spandagou have identified what they see as a fundamental difference in understandings of 'inclusion' and 'inclusive education' between '. . . the countries of the North and of the South' [p. 29].)

Trainee teachers

Like the UK study outlined above, Australian research has demonstrated comprehensively that trainee teachers exhibit a wide variety of views about various manifestations of diversity and an equally wide variety of attitudes towards strategies for celebrating that diversity and including it successfully in formal educational practice. These sites of diversity and inclusion – and sometimes exclusion – range from disabilities (Forlin & Chambers, 2011; Raphael & Allard, 2012/in press) and special educational needs (Graham & Jahnukainen, 2011; see also Woodcock, Hemmings, & Kay, 2012) to language (Nuttall & Ortlipp, 2012) and multiculturalism (Burnett & McArdle, 2011; Reid & Sriprakash, 2012) to sexuality (Robinson & Ferfolja, 2008) and social justice (Mills, 2012).

Australian research has also highlighted the complexity of efforts to assist trainee teachers to engage effectively and wholeheartedly with issues of diversity and inclusion in their training programmes and in their teaching endeavours. Indeed, it follows from that complexity that there needs to be equivalent diversity in approaches to such training. For instance, from an international dataset including from Australia, Forlin, Loreman, Sharma and Earle (2009) identified '. . . the effect of a range of demographic differences on changing pre-service teacher attitudes toward inclusion; [and] sentiments

towards people with a disability and in reducing their concerns about inclusion
...' (p. 195), and they emphasized '. . . the importance of differentiating teacher
preparation courses to address these different needs of pre-service teachers'
(p. 195).

At the same time, teacher training programmes have developed specialist
courses in Australia, as they have done in the UK, that are claimed from varied
perspectives to contribute positively to trainee teachers' understandings of
diversity and inclusion issues. For example, Maher (2012/in press) reported a
teacher training innovation that enabled Indigenous Australian assistant teachers
to work closely with non-Indigenous teachers in their respective communities to
become qualified teachers in their own right. Likewise Lancaster and Bain (2010)
indicated that both a field-based placement and '. . . course design approach
derived from complex adaptive systems' (p. 117) yielded statistically significant
increases in the self-efficacy of primary school trainee teachers identified as
having inclusive educational needs. Similarly, Ballantyne and Mills (2008) used
interviews during teacher training and six months into the first year of teaching
with six music teachers to explain how pre-service music teacher education can
generate sustainable practices for promoting socially just and inclusive music
education.

Moreover, incorporating extended experiences of service learning in multiple
community sites outside the academy were found to enhance trainee teachers'
development of '. . . sophisticated understandings of pedagogy in diverse contexts
for diverse learners' (Ryan, Carrington, Selva, & Healy, 2009, p. 155; Ryan & Healy,
2009). A couple of representative quotations by trainee teachers involved in
these service learning experiences reflected their growing understanding of the
complexity of diversity and inclusion, as well as their determination to pursue
these goals when they became teachers in their own right:

> Without patience, loving care, and the notion of being inclusive, none
> of these children would be able to survive in this world. I will teach my
> students that inclusivity and diversity are a large part of learning. I know I
> will struggle to achieve all that I want to achieve in inclusive teaching but I
> will be a reflective learning. (as cited by Carrington, 2011, p. 9)

> In future teaching, I need to advocate the rights of my students, and try to
> obtain funding so that they are not excluded because of their family's socio-
> economic circumstance. As a first year teacher, one of my aims is to be as
> proactive as possible and advocate for the rights and needs of the students
> in my classroom and community. I believe I have gained an increased

awareness in helping all the students I come into contact with. (as cited by Carrington, 2011, p. 9)

Tutors

There is also a growing body of empirical research in Australia focused on the aspirations and experiences of tutors of trainee teachers, generally known in Australia as 'teacher educators'. One critical incident that was reported (Danaher, Gale, & Erben, 2000) as encapsulating broader issues about diversity and inclusion related to Australians' continuing ambivalence about 'Asia' (in itself a vast continent containing significant cultural and linguistic diversities). The incident pertained to an Australian government policy at the time to promote Australian undergraduates' opportunities to spend time studying in one or more Asian countries, in order to enhance their understandings of those countries and to increase Australia's profile in those countries. As part of the same programme, trainee teachers and graduate teachers arrived at the Australian university in question for periods of varying duration to experience 'Australian culture' and to learn about Australian schooling systems. Yet their arrival presented the Australian tutors with a dilemma:

> There are some teacher educators in the faculty who are literate in the visitors' cultural understandings and are able to draw on both 'western' and 'eastern' ideas in ways that are both relevant to these students' needs. However, other faculty members appear to have neither the skills nor the resources to engage with these exchanges in ways that would reciprocally expand or internalise the knowledge of either the teachers-in-training or themselves. What could be fruitful cross-cultural academic interactions among individuals from very different countries remain at best, and for the most part, perfunctory, cursory and superficial. (p. 59)

More broadly, this dilemma accentuated a deeper concern related to Australian teacher training: the need:

> . . . to focus on rethinking its knowledge base – how it is assembled, represented and imparted. This is important for all Australian teacher educators, in order better to service the needs not simply of international students (those from overseas who study in Australia) but also of internalised students (Australian student teachers who undertake parts of their courses overseas). (Danaher, Gale, & Erben, 2000, p. 60)

Even more widely, this dilemma highlighted the crucial roles and responsibilities of tutors as potential agents of transformation and/or replication of the status quo with regard to diversity and inclusion. At the individual tutor level, the pressures are significant and often stressful:

> Such revisioning will involve more than simply responding to students' languages and ethnicities, and teacher educators can teach only what they know. Not knowing as well as not being committed to the Asian 'other', for example, will mean that the potential internationalisation of Australian teacher education will continue to be frustrated. (Danaher, Gale, & Erben, 2000, p. 60)

Yet clearly individual tutors need to be assisted and supported in their efforts to engage proactively and productively with issues of diversity and inclusion, and that in turn generates additional responsibilities for teacher training institutions as well as for government departments and registration authorities.

As with the UK study reported above, the Australian research into trainee teachers' and tutors' understandings of racialized identities, and more broadly of diversity and inclusion issues, reinforces anew what a set of troubling terrains (Henderson & Danaher, 2008) this field of higher education is. Trainee teachers and their tutors vary widely in relation to what diversity and inclusion are and mean, and the strategies most likely to address these issues and achieve these goals. In doing so, they demonstrate again that the links between identity and pedagogy in this field of higher education are often ill-defined and even tenuous rather than clear and direct. Individual trainees and tutors sometimes express a sense of feeling overwhelming by the size of the task confronting them and other participants in the educational enterprise. Yet much of the research – in Australia as much as in the UK – provides strong evidence of the respondents' resilience against considerable odds and of their determination to continue doing what they can to enhance the educational experiences and outcomes of their variously marginalized pupils.

Notes

1   All names of respondents are pseudonyms.
2   The *Daily Mail* is a right-wing, tabloid newspaper published daily in the UK. It is the second biggest selling daily newspaper after the *Sun*. Its founder, Lord Rothermere, was a friend and supporter of Benito Mussolini and Adolf Hitler, which has historically influenced the *Daily Mail*'s political stance.

3   The British National Party (BNP) is a far right political party that was formed by
    John Tyndall in 1982 as a splinter group of the National Front. The BNP restricted its
    membership to 'indigenous British' people until a legal challenge to its constitution
    in 2010. It has a history of inciting racial hatred and has been described by the
    European Parliament as an 'openly Nazi party'. Its own members have described the
    party as follows: 'We are 100% racist' (BNP Under the Skin, BBC 2007).

4   The *Every Child Matters* (ECM) Agenda is a UK government initiative that was set
    up in 2003; it led to the introduction of *The Children Act* in 2004. The ECM Agenda
    works within a multi-agency partnership to ensure that all children, regardless of
    their backgrounds, are entitled to have the support that they need to be safe and
    healthy, achieve to their full potential, make a positive contribution to society and
    achieve economic well-being.

7

Conclusions

The book concludes by bringing together the previous discussions of 'race' and identities and proposes a new way forward from which to engage with racialized identities in higher education by focusing on research, policy and practice, in pre-service teacher training specifically and higher education more widely. This proposal is particularly informed by the book's comparative analysis of a national and international perspective, drawing on the commonalities and differences between the UK and Australia. The chapter also considers how professional higher educators and teacher trainers can understand issues of identities to engage with the multiple educational aspirations and outcomes of minority ethnic groups.

Summary of findings

We have sought in this book to do a number of things. We have examined the key concepts – and the associated issues – of 'race', identity and gender, particularly as they intersect with, and help to explain, the experiences of students in higher education, particularly in teacher training programmes. We have presented those concepts, issues and experiences by means of a theoretically grounded comparison between local and international university students in the UK and Australia. That comparison has emphasized the continuing influence of the respective higher education system in the two countries, as well as the ongoing impact of the different national, local and institutional contexts on the kinds of education experienced by specific minority ethnic groups. We have also interrogated the status of higher education as a vehicle for productive change for those groups vis-à-vis its role in replicating the sources of their marginalization, against the broader backdrop of the controversial debates surround 'race', gender and class inequalities in both countries.

More specifically, we introduced the book by situating it within a wider body of scholarship, drawn in this case mainly from the UK, the USA and Australia, related to the educational experiences, and particularly the continuing disparities in educational access and outcomes, of variously marginalized individuals and groups. The discussion was clustered around the key organizing notions of multiculturalism, social justice, diversity and inclusion.

In Chapter 1, we examined selected key debates about identity, 'race', gender and culture within the UK and the Australian contexts. We highlighted that, separately and in combination, these debates are complex, contested and controversial, and that argument remains about their definitions, meanings, causes and effects. We also contended that despite that argument they undoubtedly exercise a profound material, psychological and sociocultural impact on the lives of members of minority ethnic and other marginalized communities.

Chapter 2 was concerned with elaborating particular theoretical understandings of the significant and vexed notion of identity. These understandings were manifested through a number of different sites, including national professional standards for teachers (and the varied requirements within those standards for teachers in both countries to demonstrate their understandings of and engagements with diverse forms of identities), national legislation related to racial and other kinds of discrimination (and the underlying theoretical assumptions about identity) and selected empirical examples of understandings of White and Black identities.

In Chapter 3, we analysed the contexts of the higher education systems in the UK and Australia and the impact of those contexts on particular enactments of identity. We explored such issues as different university types, university groupings, debates around widening participation, who goes to university, the impact of tuition fees and higher education's putative business status. In combination, these issues constitute a complex institutional framework with which minority ethnic students must engage intelligently and wholeheartedly if they are to achieve success (however such success is defined and measured).

Chapter 4 considered the complex and crucial question of educational identities in the UK and Australia (with some comparative material from the USA). This question was organized in terms of White and Black educational identities and their respective intersections with CRT and with formal educational provision.

In Chapter 5, we elaborated some of the key methodological and ethical difficulties and associated strategies in designing and conducting research about racialized identities in the UK and Australia. These difficulties and strategies included gaining access, sensitive research and power differentials, and they have continuing implications for researcher identities and researching identities.

Chapter 6 presented a necessarily lengthy analysis of empirical data about students' understandings – particularly those of trainee teachers – of racialized identities in the UK and Australia. These understandings were clustered around such concepts as diversity and inclusion, and also included 'race', Whiteness and Blackness, and class and locality. Selected perspectives of teacher trainers were included as well, to complement and augment the positions articulated by the students.

Implications for research, policy and practice

Research

This book is partly a research book, drawing as it has done on our own and others' conceptual and empirical data gathering and analysis conducted across a large number and a wide range of educational research projects. In many ways the previous chapter has highlighted the strengths as well as the inevitable limitations of such research. The strengths include emphasizing the diversity of understandings of and views about the contested and often troubling terrains (Henderson & Danaher, 2008) of racialized identities, as well as painting frequently vivid pen pictures of respondents' opinions and their struggles to engage with competing pressures and priorities. The limitations include the difficulties associated with generalizing interpretations from individual understandings and with generating effective policies and guidelines from them. The limitations also include a concern (also noted in Chapter 5) that participants in interviews and questionnaire surveys about such sensitive topics might respond in ways that they feel that the researcher/s would like them to respond rather than in terms of what they actually believe, as well as the potential mismatch between what participants say (whether authentically or artificially) on the one hand and what they do in practice on the other. Certainly further research in this field of students' and staff members' understandings of racialized identities in higher education, and particularly in teacher training, is warranted.

Likewise, on the basis of our research reported here, we recommend in both our countries a national research project to examine all ITT providers to explore whether and how they are teaching courses related to 'race', diversity and inclusion, with a view both to adding information about the courses to the national and international store of scholarship about such matters and to influencing educational policy-making in education at the local/state, national and international levels. These research-based strategies would contribute significantly to the knowledge base about how trainee teachers understand social justice and multiculturalism and about how inclusion can be implemented successfully in the classroom.

Additional internationally comparative research, of the kind attempted in this book, is also warranted. This is despite the difficulties that we have encountered, both theoretical (in terms of having a common and clearly defined conceptual framework so that we were writing about the same phenomena in our respective countries) and methodological (the sheer complexity of the contexts framing higher education and teacher training in our two countries). The onrush of globalization notwithstanding, mapping and analysing highly diverse contexts at varying levels (international, national, regional, local, institutional and individual) are crucial tasks if we are to understand and to be able to engage effectively with the complexity and diversity of racialized identities. International comparisons of this type are a significant part of that mapping and analysis.

Policy and practice

Our research suggests strongly that trainee teachers and their tutors should have a greater understanding of issues to do with 'race', diversity and inclusion in order to develop a proactive, sustainable and potentially transformative social justice agenda in schools and in education. The more knowledge and expertise that trainee teachers have about understanding 'race', diversity and inclusion and what these concepts mean in relation to pupils' experiences, the better equipped that they will be to deal with racism in the classroom, counter racist attitudes and move on to developing an inclusive teaching agenda. These measures will also have implications for future policy and practice in all aspects of education.

Our research has certainly found that the majority of respondents had some understanding of the key issues of 'race', diversity and inclusion, and that they were able to apply this to their own teaching. On the other hand, this understanding was generally based on their own experiences, rather than what they had been taught in their teacher training courses. Few of the trainee teachers said that an understanding of these key issues was not a priority before they joined the course. However, once they started on the course, they became aware that knowledge of 'race', diversity and inclusion issues was vital to all aspects of their teaching – whether this was a focus of their concern or not. The majority (indeed, almost all) of the trainee teachers felt that the teaching of these issues should be central to teacher training and should be a focus of all aspects of subject knowledge.

More specifically, all respondents stressed the importance of greater input via courses to do with 'race', diversity and inclusion, particularly practical sessions (with real-life case-study examples) about how to deal with racism in the classroom (including countering the use of racist language). Participants indicated that such courses should be compulsory for *all* trainee teachers regardless of whether they were teaching in early childhood settings, primary or secondary schools or further education. The findings further suggest that future educational policy-making should include a compulsory course on 'race', diversity and inclusion for trainee teachers, how these concepts are defined and their relationship to issues of racism, exclusion and marginalization.

There is also a need for continuous professional development for tutors that should include legal updates on diversity issues and equal opportunities. There should also be a regular assessment of how tutors are teaching such issues to trainee teachers and an examination of the particular challenges that they are facing in the current social and political climates. An emphasis on how tutors can improve their teaching, through the sharing of 'good practice', could form the basis of the courses and the different strategies used in teaching them.

More broadly, the book contributes to ongoing policy and practice debates about higher education access and provision. The recent introduction of university fees in the UK has highlighted diverse views about whether higher education should be seen as a right, a privilege, a service or a commodity. McCowan (2012) contends that '. . . a right to higher education [should be] seen as one of a number of possible forms of post-school education, restricted only a requirement for a minimum level of academic preparation' (p. 111), thereby blending human rights and meritocratic discourses. Yet the findings of this book suggest that other barriers to higher education access exist that are less visible and less amenable to policy intervention, but that are more powerful and enduring, than the imposition of student fees. These barriers relate to the intersection between identity and pedagogy for ethnic minority groups, both in higher education and in other formal educational settings. It is vital to continue to seek means of moving towards a new way – or several new ways simultaneously –

forward on the research, policy and practice fronts if these barriers are to be challenged and potentially to be overcome.

Towards a new way forward: Identity and pedagogy in higher education

This final section of the chapter – and of the book – is necessarily provisional and tentative. At the same time, it derives from the concern and conviction that we both feel – as do many of the participants in the research projects reported in the previous chapter – that more can and should be done at multiple levels to continue to engage with the complex and diverse phenomena of racialized identities as they intersect with and impact on pedagogy, higher education and teacher training.

In particular, we have distilled four specific themes that for us encapsulate some of the key issues, and some of the associated possibilities, emerging from the preceding chapters of the book. There are lots of others, of course, but we contend that little progress will be made if these four themes are not addressed. Moreover, we have presented this distillation by means of posing five organizing questions for each theme, derived from the previous chapters, under each theme. Again these questions are seen as representative rather than as comprehensive, but they should provide a starting point for seeking a new way forward in these vital areas.

Identity

- What are the commonalities and contradictions between particular manifestations of identity (such as 'race', gender and class)?
- How are multiple dimensions of identity experienced by individuals, groups and communities on a daily basis?
- What kinds of strategies do individuals, groups and communities enact in order to celebrate and/or to disguise specific aspects of their identity?
- What do higher educators and teacher trainers need to know and to be able to do to engage appropriately and ethically with the identity constructions and strategies of variously marginalized groups?
- How can educational researchers increase the relevance and utility of their research into identity?

Pedagogy

- What is pedagogy and why is it important in different educational settings?
- To what extent does pedagogy as it is currently practised in higher education attract, recruit and retain members of variously marginalized groups?
- Which forms of pedagogy are most effective in teacher training courses in informing trainee teachers about issues of 'race', diversity and inclusion?
- Which kinds of pedagogy should current and future teachers in classroom settings implement to maximize their classrooms as places of inclusion and transformation?

Higher education

- What are the historical constituents of higher education and how have they influenced the character and impact of current higher education systems?
- In what ways are those systems welcoming of and/or hostile towards members of variously marginalized groups?
- What kinds of strategies can higher education managers and teachers implement to maximize higher education institutions as inclusive teaching and learning environments?
- How can higher education researchers contribute meaningfully to ways of enhancing higher education institutions as inclusive teaching and learning environments?

Teacher training

- To what extent, and in what ways, should teacher training be directed at replicating the status quo in the broader society versus contributing to change and transform that society?
- How can all trainee teachers be supported in increasing their understandings of racialized identities and issues of diversity and inclusion?
- How can tutors and course leaders be assisted in teaching about racialized identities and issues of diversity and inclusion?
- How can members of minority ethnic groups and other marginalized communities be encouraged to begin and complete teacher training courses and to become longstanding and productive members of the teaching profession?

Many of the ideas and issues portrayed in this book are far from easy to implement and even to discuss. If racial equality – however that is understood – were a straightforward goal to attain, it would have been achieved long ago. Instead the racialized dimensions of identity continue to challenge the understandings and tax the determination and goodwill of individuals, groups and communities of minority as well as majority ethnic status.

Certainly higher education institutions and teacher training courses remain sites of unwitting – and sometimes of intentional – marginalization and racism. Equally certainly it behoves all of us – trainee teachers, tutors, teachers, pupils, administrators and researchers – to continue to explore, and to seek to find new ways forward, in relation to the complex intersections among identity, pedagogy, higher education and teacher training, whether in the UK, Australia or elsewhere in the world today.

References

Acker, A. (2008). Making the multicultural learning environment flourish. *Australian Journal of Early Childhood, 33*(1), 9–16.

Ahmad, F., Modood, T., & Lissenburgh, S. (2003). *South Asian women and employment in Britain: The interaction of gender and ethnicity.* London: PSI.

Ainley, P., & Allen, M. (2010). *Lost generation: New strategies for youth and education.* London: Continuum.

Ali, L., & Sonn, C. C. (2009, June). Multiculturalism and whiteness: Through the experiences of second generation Cypriot Turkish. *Australian Community Psychologist, 21*(1), 24–38.

— (2010, September). Constructing identity as a second-generation Cypriot Turkish in Australia: The multi-hyphenated other. *Culture Psychology, 16*(3), 416–36.

Allard, A., & Santoro, N. (2006). Troubling identities: Teacher education students' constructions of class and ethnicity. *Cambridge Journal of Education, 36*(1), 115–29.

Allen, D. (2010). Remedying discrimination: The limits of the law and the need for a systematic approach. *University of Tasmania Law Review, 29*(2), 83–110.

Altman, J. C., Biddle, N., & Hunter, B. H. (2008, October). *How realistic are the prospects for 'closing the gaps' in socioeconomic outcomes for Indigenous Australians? (CAEPR discussion paper no. 287).* Canberra, ACT, Australia: Centre for Aboriginal Economic Policy Research, College of Arts and Social Sciences, Australian National University. Retrieved from http://caepr.anu.edu.au/Publications/DP/2008DP287.php

Ambe, E. (2006). Fostering multicultural appreciation in pre-service teachers through multicultural curricular transformation. *Teaching and Teacher Education, 22*(6), 690–9.

Anderson, P., & Williams, J. (2001). Identity and difference: Concepts and themes. In P. Anderson & J. Williams (Eds.), *Identity and difference in higher education.* Aldershot: Ashgate.

Anscombe, A. W. (2010). Indigenous rural identity in Australia: From tribesman to prisoner. *Rural Society, 20*, 43–57.

Anteliz, E. A., Coombes, P. N., & Danaher, P. A. (Eds.) (2006, October). *Marginalised pedagogues?: International studies of the work and identities of contemporary educators teaching 'minority' learners.* Theme issue of *Teaching and Teacher Education, 22*(7), 753–837.

Anthias, F. (2008). Thinking through the lens of translocational positionality: An intersectionality frame for understanding identity and belonging. *Translocations: Migration and Social Change, 4*(1), 4–19.

Apple, M. (2006). *Educating the right way*. London and New York: Routledge.

Archer, L., & Leathwood, C. (2003). Identities, inequalities and higher education. In L. Archer, M. Hutchings, & A. Ross (Eds.), *Higher education and social class: Issues of exclusion and inclusion*. London and New York: RoutledgeFalmer.

Armstrong, D., Armstrong, A. C., & Spandagou, I. (2011). Inclusion: By choice or by name? *International Journal of Inclusive Education, 15*(1), 29–39.

Au, W. (2009). *Unequal by design: High-stakes testing and the standardization of inequality*. New York: Routledge.

Augoustinos, M., & Every, D. (2011, May). Accusations and denials of racism: Managing moral accountability in public discourse. *Discourse & Society, 21*(3), 251–6.

Australian Commonwealth Attorney-General's Department. (2011, September). *Consolidation of Commonwealth anti-discrimination laws: Discussion paper*. Canberra, ACT, Australia: Author. Retrieved from www.ag.gov.au/ Humanrightsandantidiscrimination/Australiashumanrightsframework/Documents/ Consolidation%20of%20Commonwealth%20Anti-Discrimination%20Laws.pdf

Australian Commonwealth Department of Education, Employment and Workplace Relations. (2010). *Summary of the 2010 higher education student statistics*. Canberra, ACT, Australia: Author. Retrieved from www.deewr.gov.au/HigherEducation/ Publications/HEStatistics/Publications/Pages/Home.aspx

Australian Commonwealth Department of Employment, Education and Training. (1990). *A fair chance for all: National and institutional planning for equity in higher education*. Canberra, ACT, Australia: Author.

Australian Education Network. (2012). Groupings of Australian universities. Retrieved from www.australian-universities.com/directory/australian-university-groupings/

Australian Qualifications Framework. (2012). *The Australian Qualifications Framework*. Retrieved from www.aqf.edu.au/AbouttheAQF/TheAQF/tabid/108/Default.aspx

Australian Taxation Office. (2012, 13 April). *HELP repayment thresholds and rates*. Canberra, ACT, Australia: Author. Retrieved from www.ato.gov.au/individuals/ content.aspx?doc=/content/8356.htm

Bagguley, P., & Hussain, Y. (2008). *Riotous citizens: Ethnic conflict in multicultural Britain*. Aldershot: Ashgate.

Baiocchi, G., & Corrado, L. (2010). The politics of habitus: Public, Blackness, and community activism in Salvador, Brazil. *Qualitative Sociology, 33*(3), 369–88.

Baird, M., Williamson, S., & Heron, A. (2012, June). Women, work and policy settings in Australia in 2011. *Journal of Industrial Relations, 54*(3), 326–42.

Ball, S. (2008). *The education debate*. Bristol: Polity Press.

Ballantyne, J., & Mills, C. (2008, June). Promoting socially just and inclusive music teacher education: Exploring perceptions of early-career teachers. *Research Studies in Music Education, 30*(1), 77–81.

Banerjee, S., & Tedmanson, D. (2010, April). Grass burning under our feet: Indigenous enterprise development in a political economy of Whiteness. *Management Learning, 41*(2), 147–65.

Banks, J., & Banks, A. (2004). *Multicultural education: Issues and perspectives.* London and New York: Routledge.

Barth, F. (1969). *Ethnic groups and boundaries: The social organisation of cultural difference.* Boston: Little Brown.

Basit, T. N. (1995). I want to go to college: British Muslim girls and the academic dimension of schooling. *Muslim Education Quarterly*, 12, 36–54.

Basit, T. N., & McNamara, O. (2004). Equal opportunities or affirmative action? The induction of minority ethnic teachers. *Journal of Education for Teaching, 30,* 97–115.

Basit, T. N., & Santoro, N. (2011). Playing the role of 'cultural expert': Teachers of ethnic difference in Britain and Australia. *Oxford Review of Education, 37*(1), 37–52.

Basit, T. N., McNamara, O., Roberts, L., Carrington, B., Maguire, M., & Woodrow, D. (2007). The bar is slightly higher: The perception of racism in teacher education. *Cambridge Journal of Education, 37,* 279–98.

Basit, T. N., Roberts, L., McNamara, O., Carrington, B., Maguire, M., & Woodrow, D. (2006). Did they jump or were they pushed? Reasons why minority ethnic trainees withdraw from initial teacher training courses. *British Educational Research Journal, 32,* 387–410.

Bauman, Z. (1991). *Modernity and the holocaust.* Bristol: Policy.

BBC (2007) (BNP Under the Skin) http://news.bbc.co.uk/hi/english/static/in_depth/ programmes/2001/bnp_special/default.stm

Beck, U. (1992). *Risk society: Towards a new modernity.* London: Sage.

Bell, C. M. (Ed.) (2011). *Blackness and disability: Critical examinations and cultural interventions.* East Lansing, MI: Michigan State University Press.

Bell, D. (1980). Brown V. Board of Education and the interest convergence dilemma. *Harvard Education Review, 93,* 518.

Berlak, A., & Moyenda, S. (2001). *Taking it personally: Racism from kindergarten to college.* Philadelphia: Temple University Press.

Bhavnani, K. K. (1993). Tracing the contours: Feminist research and feminist objectivity. *Women's Studies International Forum, 16*(2), 95.

Bhopal, K. (2008). Shared communities and shared understandings: The experiences of Asian women in a British university. *International Studies in Sociology of Education, 18*(3 & 4), 185–97.

— (2009). Identity, empathy and 'otherness': Asian women, education and dowries in the UK. (In special issue: Black Feminisms and postcolonial paradigms: Researching educational inequalities). *Race Ethnicity and Education, 12*(1), 27–39.

— (2010). *Asian women in higher education: Shared communities.* Stoke-on-Trent: Trentham.

Bhopal, K., & Myers, M. (2008). *Insiders, outsiders and others: Gypsies and identity.* Hatfield, UK: University of Hertfordshire Press.

Bhopal, K., & Preston, J. (Eds.) (2011). *Intersectionality and 'race' in education.* New York, US and London: Routledge.

Bhopal, K., & Takhar, S. (2010). *The motivations and choices of South Asian and Black Caribbean women in higher education*. In British Educaitonal Research Association Annual Conference, Warwick, 1–4 September 2010.

Bhopal, K., Harris, R., & Rhamie, J. (2009). *The teaching of 'race', diversity and inclusion on PGCE courses: A case study analysis of University of Southampton*. Multiverse, TDA.

Billett, S. (2009). Conceptualizing learning experiences: Contributions and mediations of the social, personal, and brute. *Mind, Culture, and Activity, 16*(10), 32–47.

Birch, E. R., & Miller, P. W. (2008). HECS: Some missing pieces. *Australian Universities Review, 50*(1), 30–6.

Blackmore, J. (2010). 'The other within': Race/Gender disruptions to the professional learning of White educational leaders. *International Journal of Leadership in Education: Theory and Practice, 13*(1), 45–61.

— (2011). Bureaucratic, corporate/market and network governance: Shifting spaces for gender equity in education. *Gender, Work & Organization, 18*(5), 443–66.

Blair, T. (2001). *Labour's education manifesto*. Speech launching Labour's education policies at the University of Southampton, UK. 23 May 2001.

Blanch, F. (2012/in press). Encountering the other: One Indigenous Australian woman's experience of racialisation on a Saturday night. *Gender, Place & Culture: A Journal of Feminist Geography*.

Bliuc, A.-M., McGarty, C., Hartley, L., & Muntele Hendres, D. (2012/in press). Manipulating national identity: The strategic use of rhetoric by supporters and opponents of the 'Cronulla riots' in Australia. *Ethnic and Racial Studies*.

Block, K., Warr, D., Gibbs, L., & Biggs, E. (2012/in press). Addressing ethical and methodological challenges in research with refugee-background young people: Reflections from the field. *Journal of Refugee Studies*.

Bloul, R. A. D. (2008). Anti-discrimination laws, Islamophobia, and ethnicization of Muslim identities in Europe and Australia. *Journal of Muslim Minority Affairs, 28*(1), 7–25.

Boese, M., & Phillips, M. (2011, April). Critical review: Multiculturalism and social inclusion in Australia. *Journal of Intercultural Studies, 32*(2), 189–97.

Bonnett, A. (1998) Situationalism geography and poststructuralism. *Environment and Planning D, 7*, 131–46.

— (2000). *Anti-racism*. London and New York: Routledge.

Bourke, T., Ryan, M., & Lidstone, J. (2012/in press). Reclaiming professionalism for geography education: Defending our own territory. *Teaching and Teacher Education*.

Bowden, M. P., & Doughney, J. (2010). Socio-economic status, cultural diversity and the aspirations of secondary students in the western suburbs of Melbourne, Australia. *Higher Education, 59*(1), 115–29.

Bradley, D., Noonan, P., Nugent, H., & Scales, B. (2008). *Review of Australian higher education: Final report*. Canberra, ACT, Australia: Department of Education, Employment and Workplace Relations.

Brah, A. (1996). *Cartographies of diaspora: Contesting identities (gender, racism, ethnicity series)*. London, UK: Routledge.

Brah, A., & Phoenix, A. (2004). 'Aint I a woman? Revisiting sexuality'. *Journal of International Women's Studies, 5*(3), 76–86.

Brookfield, S. (1995). *Becoming a critically reflective teacher*. San Francisco, CA: Jossey-Bass.

Brown, L. (2010). Nurturing relationships within a space created by 'Indigenous ways of knowing': A case study. *Australian Journal of Indigenous Education, 39* (supplement), 15–22.

Burnett, B., & McArdle, F. (2011). Multiculturalism, education for sustainable development (EST) and the shifting discursive landscape of social inclusion. *Discourse: Studies in the Cultural Politics of Education, 32*(1), 43–56.

Butler, J. (1990). *Gender trouble: Feminism and the subversion of identity*. London and New York: Routledge.

Calcutt, L., Woodward, I., & Skrbis, Z. (2009, June). Conceptualizing otherness: An exploration of the cosmopolitan schema. *Journal of Sociology, 45*(2), 169–86.

Caluya, G., Probyn, E., & Vyas, S. (2011). 'Affective eduscapes': The case of Indian students within Australian international higher education. *Cambridge Journal of Education, 41*(1), 85–99.

Campbell, R., & Wasco, S. M. (2000). Feminist approaches to social science: Epistemological and methodological tenets. *American Journal of Community Psychology*, 28(6), 773–91.

Carby, H. (1982). White woman listen! Black Feminism and the boundaries of sisterhood. *The Empire strikes back: Race and racism in seventies Britain* (pp. 212–35). London: Hutchinson.

Carey, J., & McLisky, C. (Eds.) (2009). *Creating White Australia*. Sydney, NSW, Australia: Sydney University Press.

Carrington, B. & Skelton, C. (2003) Re-thinking 'role models': Equal opportunities in teacher recruitment in England and Wales. *Journal of Education Policy, 18*(3), 253–65.

Carrington, B., Bonnett, A., Demaine, J., Hall, I., Nayak, A., Short, G., . . . Tomlin, R. (2001). *Report to the teacher training agency – Ethnicity and the professional socialisation of teachers*: Available online at: www.tta.gov.uk/asets/about/recruit/tsr/carringtonrep/newcastle_research.pdf

Carrington, S. (2011, May). Service-learning within higher education: Rhizomatic interconnections between university and the real world. *Australian Journal of Teacher Education, 36*(6), article 1.

Carson, T. (2009, April). A history of equity in higher education in Australia: Making universities more accessible for students from disadvantaged backgrounds. *Widening Participation and Lifelong Learning, 11*(1), 5–16.

Causey, V. E., Thomas, C. D., & Armento, B. J. (2000). Cultural diversity is basically a foreign term to me: The challenges of diversity for pre-service teacher education. *Teaching and Teacher Education*, 16, 33–45.

Choy, S. C., Bowman, K., Billett, S., Wignall, L., & Haukka, S. (2008). *Effective models of employment-based training (technical report)*. Adelaide, SA, Australia: National Centre for Vocational Education Research. Retrieved from http://eprints.qut.edu.au/13630/1/13630.pdf

Chubbuck, S. M. (2010). Individual and structural orientations in socially just teaching: Conceptualization, implementation, and collaborative effort. *Journal of Teacher Education, 61*(3), 197–210.

Clarke, M., & Drudy, S. (2007). Social justice in initial teacher education: Student teachers' reflections on praxis. In C. Gaine, G. Bhatti, Y. Leeman, & F. Gobbo (Eds.), *Social justice and intercultural education: An open ended dialogue*. Stoke-on-Trent: Trentham.

Clausen, M., & Anderson, M. (2012). Crossing borders: Reading Indigenous playtexts in White classrooms. In J. Manuel & S. Brindley (Eds.), *Teenagers and reading: Literary heritages, cultural contexts and contemporary reading practices (Australian Association for the Teaching of English interface series)* (pp. 176–90). Kent Town, SA, Australia: Wakefield Press.

Cochran-Smith, M. (2000). Blind vision: Unlearning racism in teacher education. *Harvard Educational Review, 70*(2), 157–90.

Cockburn, A. D., & Haydn, T. (2004). *Recruiting and retaining teachers: Understanding why teachers teach*. London: RoutledgeFalmer.

Cockrell, K. S., Placier, P. L., Cockrell, D. H., & Middleton, J. N. (1999). Coming to terms with 'diversity' and 'multiculturalism' in teacher education: Learning about our students, changing our practice. *Teaching and Teacher Education, 15*, 351–66.

Cole, M. (2009). Racism and education in the UK and US. London: Palgrave.

Cole, M., & Maisuria, A. (2010). Racism and Islamophobia in post 7/7 Britain: Critical race theory, (xeno-) racialization, empire and education: A Marxist analysis. In D. Kelsh, D. Hill, & S. Macrine (Eds.), *Class in education: Knowledge, pedagogy, subjectivity*. New York: Routledge.

Cole, M., & Stuart, J. (2005). 'Do you ride on elephants?' and 'Never tell them you are German': The experiences of British Asian and Black, and overseas student teachers in Southeast England. *British Educational Research Journal, 31*(3), 349–66.

Colic-Peisker, V., & Tilbury, F. (2008, April). Being Black in Australia: A case study of intergroup relations. *Race Class, 49*(4), 38–56.

Collins, P. H. (2005). *Black sexual politics: African Americans, gender and the new racism*. London and New York: Routledge.

Connell, R. (2008). Masculinity construction and sports in boys' education: A framework for thinking about the issue. *Sport, Education and Society, 13*(2), 131–45.

Coombes, P. N., Danaher, G. R., & Danaher, P. A. (forthcoming). Mobile performance spaces: Learning by mobile communities, non-traditional university students and retirees. Frankfurt, Germany: Peter Lang.

Cotterill, P. (1992). Interviewing women: Issues of friendship, vulnerability, and power. *Women's Studies International Forum, 15*, 593–606.

Couch, J. (2011). A new way home: Refugee young people and homelessness in Australia. *Journal of Social Inclusion, 2*(1), 39–52.

Cox, E. (2011). 'What's past is prologue': Performing Shakespeare and Aboriginality in Australia. *Multicultural Shakespeare: Translation, Appropriation and Performance, 8*(8), 71–92.

Crenshaw, K. (1989). Demarginalizing the intersection of race and sex: A Black Feminist critique of antidiscrimination doctrine, Feminist theory and antiracist politics. *University of Chicago Legal Forum,* 139–67.

— (1991). Mapping the margins: Intersectionality, identity politics, and violence against women of color. *Stanford Law Review, 43,* 1241–99.

Crichton, J., & Scarino, A. (2007). How are we to understand the 'intercultural dimension'? An examination of the intercultural dimension of internationalisation in the context of higher education in Australia. *Australian Review of Applied Linguistics, 30*(1), 04.1–04.21.

Crockett, D. (2008, July). Marketing blackness: How advertises use race to sell products. *Journal of Consumer Culture, 8*(2), 245–68.

Crowley, V., & Rasmussen, M. L. (2010). After dark in the antipodes: Pedagogy, place and queer phenomenology. *International Journal of Qualitative Studies in Education, 23*(1), 15–32.

Daily Telegraph (2009). Trevor Phillips warns that Britain could return to racism as recession bites.

Danaher, P. A. (1991, January). *The coming of the light: The response of the Darnley Islanders to the London Missionary Society, 1871–1914.* Unpublished Master of Letters dissertation. Armidale, NSW, Australia: University of New England.

— (1998). Ethics and researching educational itinerancy. In P. A. Danaher (Ed.), *Beyond the ferris wheel: Educating Queensland show children (Studies in open and distance learning number 1)* (pp. 57–69). Rockhampton, Qld, Australia: Central Queensland University Press.

— (2001, March). *Learning on the run: Traveller education for itinerant show children in coastal and western Queensland.* Unpublished Doctor of Philosophy dissertation. Rockhampton, Qld, Australia: Faculty of Education and Creative Arts, Central Queensland University.

Danaher, P. A., & Danaher, G. R. (1993–4). *An evaluation of three Aboriginal and Torres Strait Islander access programs (CNJ62 Certificate of Basic Education; CNJ63 Certificate of General studies; CNJ65 Certificate of Vocational Preparation) in Queensland Colleges of Technical and Further Education.* Rockhampton, Qld, Australia: Central Queensland University.

Danaher, P. A., & Umar, A. (Eds.) (2010, September). *Teacher education through open and distance learning (Perspectives on distance education).* Vancouver, BC: Commonwealth of Learning.

Danaher, P. A., Coombes, P. N., & Kiddle, C. (2007). *Teaching traveller children: Maximising learning outcomes.* Stoke-on-Trent: Trentham.

Danaher, P. A., Gale, T. C., & Erben, T. (2000, April). The teacher educator as (re)negotiated professional: Critical incidents in steering between state and market in Australia. *Journal of Education for Teaching, 26*(1), 55–71.

Danaher, P. A., Moriarty, B. J., & Danaher, G. R. (2009). *Mobile learning communities: Creating new educational futures.* New York, NY: Routledge.

Darling-Hammond, L., & Bransford, J. (2005). *Preparing teachers for a changing world.* San Francisco: Jossey-Bass.

Davies, J., & Crozier, G. (2006). *Diversity and teacher education: Research into training provision in England: End of project report.* Available online on the Multiverse website: www.multiverse.ac.uk/attachments/80812ad2–6f70–4470-b632-f65c10a70b3b.doc

Day, D., & Nolde, R. (2009). Arresting the decline in Australian Indigenous representation at university: Student experience as a guide. *Equal Opportunities International, 28*(2), 135–61.

Delgado, R., & Stefanic, S. (2000). *Critical Race Theory: An introduction.* London and New York: Routledge.

Denson, N., & Zhang, S. (2010). The impact of student experiences with diversity on developing graduate attributes. *Studies in Higher Education, 35*(5), 529–43.

Department for Education and Science(DfES) (2003). *The Future of higher education.*

— (2006). *Ethnicity and education.*

— (2007). *Gender and education.*

Desforges, C. (1995). *An introduction to teaching psychological perspectives.* Springer: Dordrecht.

Devlin, M., & O'Shea, H. (2012/in press). Effective university teaching: Views of Australian university students from low socio-economic status backgrounds. *Teaching in higher education.*

Dolby, N. E. (2005, April). Globalisation, identity and nation: Australian and American undergraduates abroad. *Australian Educational Researcher, 32*(1), 101–17.

Donaldson, G. (2001). *Cultivating leadership in schools.* Williston: Teachers College Press.

Douglas, D. D. (2012, March). Venus, Serena, and the inconspicuous consumption of Blackness: A commentary on surveillance, race talk, and new racism(s). *Journal of Black Studies, 43*(2), 127–45.

Downing, R., & Kowal, E. (2011). A postcolonial analysis of Indigenous cultural awareness training for health workers. *Health Sociology Review, 20*(1), 5–15.

Dunn, K. M., Pelleri, D., & Maeder-Han, K. (2011, April). Attacks on Indian students: The commerce of denial in Australia. *Race & Class, 52*(4), 71–88.

Dunn, K. M., Forrest, J., Pe-Pua, R., Hynes, M., & Maeder-Han, K. (2009). Cities of race hatred? The spheres of racism and anti-racism in contemporary Australian cities. *Cosmopolitan Civil Societies: An Interdisciplinary Journal, 1*(1), 1–14.

Dunne, C. (2011). Developing an intercultural curriculum within the context of the internationalisation of higher education: Terminology, typologies and power. *Higher Education Research & Development, 30*(5), 609–22.

Durey, A. (2010, July). Reducing racism in Aboriginal health care in Australia: Where does cultural education fit? *Australian and New Zealand Journal of Public Health, 34*(S1), S87–S92.

Dyer, R. (1997). *White: Essays on race and culture*. London and New York: Routledge.

Every, D., & Augoustinos, M. (2008, July). Constructions of Australia in pro- and anti-asylum seeker political discourse. *Nations and Nationalism, 14*(3), 562–80.

Federation of Islamic Studies (2005). *Islam on Campus* by Centre for Social Cohesion. London 2008.

Ferfolja, T. (2009). The refugee action support program: Developing understandings of diversity. *Teaching Education, 20*(4), 395–407.

Fitzgerald, L. K. (2010, December). An investigation of Indigenous participation in a business degree programme. *Widening Participation and Lifelong Learning, 12*(3), 19–35.

Fontana, A., & Frey, J. H. (2005). The interview: From neutral stance to political involvement. In N. K. Denzin & Y. S. Lincoln (Eds.), *The SAGE handbook of qualitative research* (pp. 695–728). Thousand Oaks, CA: Sage.

Forlin, C., & Chambers, D. (2011). Teacher preparation for inclusive education: Increasing knowledge but raising concerns. *Asia-Pacific Journal of Teacher Education, 39*(1), 17–32.

Forlin, C., Loreman, T., Sharma, U., & Earle, C. (2009). Demographic differences in changing pre-service teachers' attitudes, sentiments and concerns about inclusive education. *International Journal of Inclusive Education, 13*(2), 195–209.

Frankenberg, R. (1993). *White woman, race matters*. London: Sage.

Fraser, N. (1997). *From redistribution to recognition*. London: Routledge.

Furlong, A., & Kelly, P. (2005, Winter). The Brazilianisation of youth transitions in Australia and the UK? *Australian Journal of Social Issues, 40*(2), 207–25.

Gale, T. (2009, 29 June–1 July). *Towards a Southern theory of higher education*. Keynote address presented at the 12th Pacific Rim first year in higher education conference, Rydges Southbank, Townsville, Qld, Australia. Retrieved from www.fyhe.com.au/past_papers/papers09/ppts/Trevor_Gale_paper.pdf

Gale, T., & Densmore, K. (2000). *Just schooling: Explorations in the cultural politics of teaching*. Buckingham, UK: Open University Press.

— (2003). Engaging teachers: *Towards a radical democratic agenda for schooling*. Maidenhead, UK: Open University Press.

Gale, T., & Tranter, D. (2011). Social justice in Australian higher education policy: An historical and conceptual account of student participation. *Critical Studies in Education, 52*(1), 29–46.

Gallagher, T. (2000). SEL4.10: *Interviews with Year 12 pupils. In the effects of the selective system of secondary education in Northern Ireland,* Volume 1. Bangor: Department of Education. (27 pages, ISBN 1 897592 61 2).

Gay, G. (2010, January/February). Acting on beliefs in teacher education for cultural diversity. *Journal of Teacher Education, 61*(1–2), 143–52.

Gazeley, L., & Dunne, M. (2007). Researching class in the classroom: Addressing the social class attainment gap in initial teacher education. *Journal of Education for Teaching: International Research and Pedagogy, 33*(4), 409–24.

Gewirtz, S. (1998). Conceptualizing social justice in education: Mapping the territory. *Journal of Educational Policy, 13*(4), 469–84.

Gibson, M. (1976). Approaches to multicultural education in the United States: Some concepts and assumptions. *Anthropology & Education Quarterly, 15*(1).

Giddens, A. (1995). *Politics and social theory*. London: Sage.

Gidley, J. M., Hampson, G. P., Wheeler, L., & Bereded-Samuel, E. (2010). From access to success: An integrated approach to quality higher education informed by social inclusion theory and practice. *Higher Education Policy, 23*, 123–47.

Gillborn, D. (2005). Education policy as an act of white supremacy: Whiteness, critical race theory and education reform. *Journal of Education Policy 20*(4), 485–505.

— (2008). Racism and education: Coincidence or conspiracy? London: Routledge.

— (2009). Risk-free racism: Whiteness and so-called 'Free Speech'. *Wake Forest Law Review, 44*(2), 535–55.

— (2010). The colour of numbers: Surveys, statistics and deficit-thinking about race and class. *Journal of Education Policy, 25*(2), 253–76.

Gillborn, D., & Gipps, C. (1996). *Recent research on the achievements of ethnic minority pupils*. London: HMSO.

Gillborn, D., & Mirza, H. (2000). *Educational inequality: Mapping race, class and gender* (HMI 232). London: OFSTED.

Gillborn, D., & Youdell, D. (2000). *Rationing education: Policy, practice, reform, and equity*. Buckingham: Open University Press.

Gilroy, P. (1987). *There aint no Black in the Union Jack*. London: Hutchinson.

— (1993). *The Black Atlantic*. London: Verso.

Goedegebuure, L., Coates, H., van der Lee, J., & Meek, V. L. (2009). Diversity in Australian higher education: An empirical analysis. *Australian Universities' Review, 51*(2), 49–61.

Gopaldas, A., & Fischer, E. (2012). Beyond gender: Intersectionality, culture, and consumer behavior. In C. C. Otnes & L. Tuncay-Zayer (Eds.), *Gender, culture, and consumer behavior* (pp. 393–410). New York, NY: Routledge.

Gordon, J. (2000). *The colour of teaching*. London: Sage.

Gorski, P. (2000). *Multicultural education and the internet: Intersections and integrations*. Boston, MA: McGraw-Hill.

Graham, L. J., & Jahnukainen, M. (2011). Wherefore art thou, inclusion? Analysing the development of inclusive education in New South Wales, Alberta and Finland. *Journal of Education Policy, 26*(2), 263–88.

Grant, C. A., & Sleeter, C. E. (2003). *Making choices for multicultural education: Five approaches to race, class and gender* (4th edition). London: Sage.

Gregory, R. G. (2009). Musing and memories on the introduction and where to next on income contingent loans. *Australian Journal of Labour Economics, 12*(2), 237–43.

Gulson, K. N., & Parkes, R. J. (2009). In the shadows of the mission: Education policy, urban space, and the 'colonial present' in Sydney. *Race Ethnicity and Education, 12*(3), 267–80.

Gunaratnam, Y. (2003). *Researching race and ethnicity*. London: Sage.

Gurin, P., Dey, E. L., Hurtado, S., & Gurin, G. (2002). Diversity and higher education: Theory and impact on educational outcomes. *Harvard Educational Review, 72*(3), 330–66.

Haberman, M., & Post, L. (2008). *Teachers for selective education*. London and New York: Routledge.

Hagan, M., & McGlynn, C. (2004). Moving barriers: Promoting learning for diversity in initial teacher education. *Journal of Intercultural Education, 15*(4), 243–52.

Hage, G. (2000). *White nation: Fantasies of White supremacy in a multicultural society*. New York, NY: Routledge.

Hall, S. (1991). The local and the global: Globalization and ethnicity and old and new identities, old and new ethnicities. In Anthony D. King (Ed.), *Culture, globalization and the world system* (pp. 19–39, 41–68). London: Macmillan.

— (1992). New ethnicities. In J. Donald & A. Rattansi (Eds.), *'Race', culture and difference* (pp. 252–60). London: Sage.

— (1996). Cultural identity and diaspora. In P. Williams & L. Chrisman (Eds.), *Colonial discourse and post-colonial theory: A reader* (pp. 392–401). London: Harvester Wheatsheaf.

— (2000). Old and new identities, old and new ethnicities. In L. Black & J. Solomos (Eds.), *Theories of race and racism: A reader* (Routledge readers in sociology) (pp. 144–53). London, UK: Routledge.

Han, J., & Singh, M. (2007). Getting world English speaking student teachers to the *Top of the Class*: Making hope for ethno-cultural diversity in teacher education robust. *Asia-Pacific Journal of Teacher Education, 35*(3), 291–309.

Harreveld, R. E., & Singh, M. (2009). Contextualising learning at the education–training–work interface. *Education + Training, 51*(2), 92–107.

Harris, V., & Marlowe, J. (2011). Hard yards and high hopes: The educational challenges of African refugee university students in Australia. *International Journal of Teaching and Learning in Higher Education, 23*(2), 186–96.

Hartigan, J. (1997). Establishing the fact of Whiteness. John Hartigan Jr. *American Anthropologist*, New Series, 99(3).

Harvey, P. W. (2009). Science, research and social change in Indigenous health – evolving ways of knowing. *Australian Health Review, 33*(4), 628–35.

Hatoss, A., & Huijser, H. (2010). Gendered barriers to educational opportunities: Resettlement of Sudanese refugees in Australia. *Gender and Education, 22*(2), 147–60.

Hattam, R., Brennan, M., Zipin, L., & Comber, B. (2009). Researching for social justice: Contextual, conceptual and methodological challenges. *Discourse: Studies in the Cultural Politics of Education, 30*(3), 303–16.

Hawkins, K. (2010). *A cry to teach for social justice: Linking early childhood education, participatory action research and children's literature.* Unpublished Doctor of Philosophy dissertation, Faculty of Education, University of Southern Queensland, Toowoomba, Qld, Australia.

Haylett, C. (2001). Illegitimate subjects?: Abject Whites, neo-liberal modernisation and middle class multiculturalism. *Environment and Planning D: Society and Space, 19*(3), 351–70.

Henderson, R., & Danaher, P. A. (Eds.) (2008). *Troubling terrains: Tactics for traversing and transforming contemporary educational research.* Teneriffe, Qld, Australia: Post Pressed.

Her Majesty's Stationery Office. (2007). *Guidance on the duty to promote community cohesion.*

Hesse-Biber, S. N., & Leckenby, D. (2004). How Feminists practice social research. In S. N. Hesse-Biber & M. L. Yaiser (Eds.), *Feminist perspectives in social research* (pp. 209–26). Oxford: Oxford University Press.

Higher Education Careers Service Unit. (2010). *What do graduates do?*

Higher Education Funding Council of England. (2010). *Annual report.*

Higher Education Statistics Agency. (2008). *Higher education statistics for the UK.*

— (2011). Higher education statistics for the UK.

Hill, J. (2008). *The everyday language of White racism.* Malden: Wiley-Blackwell.

Holden, C. (2003). Education for global citizenship: The knowledge, understanding and motivation of trainee teachers. In A. Ross (Ed.), *A Europe of many cultures.* London: Routledge.

Hollins, E. R., & Guzman, M. T. (2005). Research on preparing teachers for divers populations. In M. Cochran-Smith & K. M. Zeichner (Eds.), *Studying teacher education: The report to the AERA panel on research and teacher education* (pp. 477–548). Mahwah, NJ: LEA.

hooks, b. (1984). *Feminist theory: From margin to center.* Boston: South End Press.

— (1992). Representing Whiteness in the Black imagination. Boston: South End Press.

Hopkins, D., West, M., & Beresford, J. (1998). Creating the conditions for classroom and teacher development. *Teachers and teaching: Theory and practice, 4*(1), 115–41.

Horsford, S. D., & Tillman, L. C. (2012, February). Inventing herself: Examining the intersectional identities and educational leadership of Black women in the USA. *International Journal of Qualitative Studies in Education, 25*(1), 1–9.

Ignatiev, N. (1995). *How the Irish became White.* London and New York: Routledge.

An Independent Review of Higher Education Funding and Student Finance (2010). *The Browne Review.*

Ingvarson, L. (2011, March). Assessing teachers for professional certification: Achieving national consistency. *Professional Educator,* 10–15. Retrieved from http://works.bepress.com/cgi/viewcontent.cgi?article=1184&context=lawrence_ingvarson1

Irvine, E. (2003). Appraisal training focused on what really matters. *International Journal of Educational Management, 17*(6), 254–61.

Jacobson, J. (1998). *Islam in Transition*. London: Routledge.

Jakubowicz, A. (2011). Chinese walls: Australian multiculturalism and the necessity for human rights. *Journal of Intercultural Studies, 32*(6), 691–706.

James, J. (2010, January). Campaigns against 'Blackness': Criminality, incivility, and election to executive office. *Critical Sociology, 36*(1), 25–44.

Jarosz, L., & Lawson, V. (2002). Sophisticated people versus Rednecks: Economic restructuring and class difference in America's West. *Antipode, 34*(1), 8–27.

Johnson, D. (2001). *Assessing outcomes-based education: A guide for teachers*. Johannesburg. Macmillan.

Johnstone, D. B., & Marcucci, P. M. (2010). *Financing higher education worldwide: Who pays? Who should pay?* Baltimore, MD: Johns Hopkins University Press.

Jorgensen (Zevenbergen), R., Grootenboer, P., Niesche, R., & Lerman, S. (2010). Challenges for teacher education: The mismatch between beliefs and practice in remote Indigenous contexts. *Asia-Pacific Journal of Teacher Education, 38*(2), 161–75.

Joseph, C. (2012, March). Internationalizing the curriculum: Pedagogy for social justice. *Current Sociology, 60*(2), 239–57.

Joseph, D., & Southcott, J. (2009). 'Opening the doors to multiculturalism': Australian pre-service music teacher education students' understandings of cultural diversity. *Music Education Research, 11*(4), 457–72.

Kamp, A., & Mansouri, F. (2010). Constructing inclusive education in a neo-liberal context: Promoting inclusion of Arab-Australian students in an Australian context. *British Educational Research Journal, 36*(5), 733–44.

Karmel, T., & Liu, S.-H. (2011). *Which paths work for which young people? (Longitudinal surveys of Australian youth research report 57)*. Adelaide, SA, Australia: National Centre for Vocational Education Research. Retrieved from http://eric.ed.gov/PDFS/ED522946.pdf

Kennedy, P. (2002). Learning cultures and learning styles. *International Journal of Lifelong Learning, 21*(5), 430–45.

Kenway, J., Bullen, E., & Robb, S. (2004). The knowledge economy, the techno-preneur and the problematic future of the university. *Policy Futures in Education, 2*(2), 330–49.

Kincheloe, J. L., & Steinberg, S. R. (1998). *Unauthorised methods: Strategies for critical teaching*. New York and London: Routledge.

Kinnear, A., Boyce, M., Sparrow, H., Middleton, S., & Cullity, M. (2008, December). *Diversity: A longitudinal study of how student diversity relates to resilience and successful progression in a new generation university: Final report*. Strawberry Hills, NSW, Australia: Australian Learning and Teaching Council. Retrieved from www.olt.gov.au/system/files/resources/CG6–38_ECU_Kinnear_Final%20Report_Apr09.pdf

Kirby, M. M., & Crawford, E. O. (2012, April). The preparation of globally competent teachers: A comparison of American and Australian education policies and perspectives. *Global Partners in Education Journal, 2*(1), 12–24.

Kitson, R., & Bowes, J. (2010, December). Incorporating Indigenous ways of knowing in early education for Indigenous children. *Australian Journal of Early Childhood, 35*(4), 81–9.

Knight, J. A., Comino, E. J., Harris, E., & Jackson-Pulver, L. (2009). Indigenous research: A commitment to walking the talk. The Gudaga study – an Australian case study. *Journal of Bioethical Inquiry, 6*(2), 467–76.

Knowles, C. (1999). Race, identity and lives. *Sociological Review, 47*(1), 110–34 .

— (2003). *Race and social analysis.* London: Sage.

Kobayashi, A., & Peake, L. (2000). Racism out of place: Thoughts on Whiteness and an antiracist geography in the new millennium. *Annals of the Association of American Geographers, 90*, 392–403.

Koerner, C. M. (2010, 5 August). *Beyond a White Australia? Race, multiculturalism, Indigenous sovereignty and Australian identities.* Unpublished Doctor of Philosophy dissertation, Centre for Development Studies, Faculty of Social and Behavioural Sciences, Flinders University of South Australia, Adelaide, SA, Australia.

Koppelman, K. L., & Goodhart, R. L. (2005). *Understanding human differences: Multicultural education for a diverse America.* Boston, MA: Pearson.

Korthagen, F. A. (2001). A reflection on reflection. In F. A. Korthagen (Ed.), *Linking practice and theory: The pedagogy of realistic teacher education* (pp. 51–68). Mahwah, NJ: Lawrence Erlbaum Associates.

Kumashiro, K. (2002). Against repetition: Addressing resistance to anti-oppressive change in the practices of learning, teaching, supervising, and researching. *Harvard Educational Review, 72*(1), 67–78.

Ladson-Billings, G. (1990). Like lightning in a bottle: Attempting to capture the pedagogical excellence of successful teachers of Black students. *International Journal of Qualitative Studies in Education, 3*, 335–44.

— (1994). *The dreamkeepers: Successful teaching for African-American students.* San Francisco: Jossey-Bass.

Ladson-Billings, G., & Gillborn, D. (2004). *The RoutledgeFalmer reader in multicultural education.* London: RoutledgeFalmer.

Lamb, N., Arizmendi, W. C., Stewart-Dore, M. N., & Danaher, P. A. (2002). Beyond Aboriginalism and culturalism in building an Indigenous-teacher lifelong-learning community: Lessons from a Torres Strait Islander distance inservice teacher-education program. In K. Appleton, C. Macpherson, & D. Orr (Eds.), *International lifelong learning conference: Refereed papers from the 2nd international lifelong learning conference Yeppoon, Central Queensland, Australia 16–19 June 2002: Hosted by Central Queensland University* (pp. 247–52). Rockhampton, Qld, Australia: Lifelong Learning Conference Committee, Central Queensland University Press.

Le Roux, J. (2002). Effective educators are culturally competent communicators. *Intercultural Education, 13*(1), 37–48.

Lea, T., Thompson, H., McRae-Williams, E., & Wegner, A. (2011). Policy fuzz and fuzzy logic: Researching contemporary Indigenous education and parent–school engagement in north Australia. *Journal of Education Policy, 26*(3), 321–39.

Leathwood, C., & Hutchings, M. (2003). Entry routes to higher education: Pathways, qualifications and social class. In L. Archer, M. Hutchings, & A. Ross (Eds.), *Higher education and social class: Issues of exclusion and inclusion* (pp. 138–54). London: RoutledgeFalmer.

Lee, W. (2002). *Equity and access to education*. Hong Kong: Comparative Education Research Centre.

Leitch Review of Skills (2006). London: HMSO.

Leonardo, Z. (2002). The souls of White folk: Critical pedagogy, Whiteness studies, and globalization discourse. *Race Ethnicity & Education, 5*(1), 29–50.

— (Ed.) (2005). *Critical pedagogy and race*. Malden, MA: Blackwell.

— (2009). *Race, Whiteness, and education*. New York: Routledge.

Letherby, G. (2003). *Feminist research in theory and practice*. London: McGraw-Hill.

Levey, G. B. (Ed.). *Political theory and Australian multiculturalism*. New York: Berghahn Books.

Lewis, J. M. (2000). *Citizenship and the new national curriculum for science*. ASE Annual Meeting.

Liamputtong, P. (2007). *Researching the vulnerable*. London: Sage.

Luxon, T., & Peelo, M. (2009). Internationalisation: Its implications for curriculum design and course development in UK higher education. *Innovations in Education and Teaching International, 46*(1), 51–60.

Mackinlay, E., & Barney, K. (2011). Teaching and learning for social justice. An approach to transformative education in Indigenous Australian studies. In G. Williams (Ed.), *Talking back, talking forward: Journeys in transforming Indigenous educational practice* (pp. 117–28). Darwin, NT, Australia: Charles Darwin University Press.

Maher, M. (2012/in press). Making inclusive education happen: The impact of initial teacher education in remote Aboriginal communities. *International Journal of Inclusive Education.*

Malone, K., Butcher, J., Howard, P., Labone, E., Bailey, M., Groundwater-Smith, S., McFadden, M., McMeniman, M., & Martinez, K. (2003). Teacher education, community service learning and student efficacy for community engagement. *Asia-Pacific Journal of Teacher Education, 31*(2), 109–24.

Mansouri, F. (2007, September). Cultural diversity as an educational advantage. *Ethnos, 15*(3), 15–18.

Mansouri, F., & Trembath, A. (2005). Multicultural education and racism: The case of Arab-Australian students in contemporary Australia. *International Education Journal, 6*(4), 516–29.

Mapedzahama, V., Rudge, T., West, S., & Perron, A. (2012, June). Black nurse in White space? Rethinking the invisibility of race within the Australian nursing workplace. *Nursing Inquiry, 19*(2), 153–64.

Marginson, S. (2004). Competition and the markets in higher education: A 'Glonacal' analysis. *Policy Futures in Education, 2*(2), 175–244.

— (2011). Global position and position-taking in higher education: The case of Australia. In S. Marginson, S. Kaur, & E. Sawir (Eds.), *Higher education in the*

Asia-Pacific: Strategic responses to globalization (Higher education dynamics vol. 36)
(pp. 375–92). Dordrecht, The Netherlands: Springer.

Marginson, S., & Considine, M. (2000). *The enterprise university: Power, governance and reinvention in Australia*. Cambridge, UK: Cambridge University Press.

Marginson, S., Nyland, C., Sawir, E., & Forbes-Mewett, H. (2010). *International student security*. Port Melbourne, Vic, Australia: Cambridge University Press.

Marks, G. N. (2009a). The social effects of the Australian Higher Education Contribution Scheme (HECS). *Higher Education, 51*(1), 71–84.

— (2009b). Modernization theory and changes over time in the reproduction of socioeconomic inequalities in Australia. *Social Forces, 88*(2), 917–44.

Markus, A. B. (2001). *Race: John Howard and the remaking of Australia*. Crows Nest, NSW, Australia: Allen & Unwin.

Markus, A. B., Jupp, J., & McDonald, P. (2009). *Australia's immigration revolution*. Sydney, NSW, Australia: Allen & Unwin.

Massey, D. (2007). *Categorically unequal: The American stratification system*. New York: Routledge.

Matereke, K. (2009, June). 'Embracing the Aussie identity': Theoretical reflections on challenges and prospects for African–Australian youths. *Australasian Review of African Studies, 30*(1), 129–43.

Matthews, J. (2008). Schooling and settlement: Refugee education in Australia. *International Studies in Sociology of Education, 18*(1), 31–45.

Maylor, U. (2009). Is it because I'm Black? A Black female research experience. *Race, Ethnicity and Education* (Special issue: 'Black feminisms and postcolonial paradigms: researching educational inequalities'), *12*(1), 53–64.

McCall, L. (2005). The complexity of intersectionality. *Signs, 3*, 1771–800.

McCowan, T. (2012). Is there a university right to higher education? *British Journal of Educational Studies, 60*(2), 111–28.

McDonald, B. L. (2005). Teacher education, training and experience: Knowing what, how, when, why and with. In I. Livingston (Ed.), *New Zealand Annual Review of Education*, 14: 2004 (pp. 21–38). Wellington, NZ: School of Educational Studies, Victoria University of Wellington.

McDonald, L. (2007). In from the cold: Developing training to impact. In K. Fanti (Ed.), *Psychological science: Research, theory and future directions* (pp. 283–96). Athens, Greece: ATINER.

McDonald., M., & Zeichner, K. (2009). Social justice teacher education. In W. Ayers, T. Quinn, & K. Stovall (Eds.), *Handbook on social justice in education*. Mahwah, NJ: Erlbaum Press.

McGlynn, C. (2003, Winter). Integrated education in Northern Ireland in the context of critical multiculturalism. *Irish Educational Studies Journal, 22*(3), 11–27.

McInerney, P., Smyth, J., & Down, B. (2011, February). 'Coming to a "place" near you?' The politics and possibilities of a critical pedagogy of place-based education. *Asia-Pacific Journal of Teacher Education, 39*(1), 3–16.

McIntosh, P. (1992). White privilege and male privilege: A personal account of coming to see correspondences through work in women's studies. In M. Andersen & P. H. Collins (Eds.), *Race, class, and gender: An anthology.* Belmont, CA: Wadsworth Publishing.

McIntyre, M. (2011). Race, surplus population and the Marxist theory of imperialism. *Antipode*, 43(5): 1489–515.

McLeod, J., & Yates, L. (2006). *Making modern lives: Subjectivity, schooling, and social change.* Albany, NY: State University of New York Press.

Mercer, K. (1994). *Welcome to the jungle: New positions in Black cultural studies.* London and New York: Routledge.

Midgley, W., Tyler, M. A., Danaher, P. A., & Mander, A. (Eds.) (2011). *Beyond binaries in education research (Routledge research in education vol. 59).* New York, NY: Routledge.

Millen, D. (1997). Some methodological and epistemological issues raised by doing Feminist research on non-Feminist women. *Sociological Research Online*, 2(3) <www.socresonline.org.uk/2/3/3.html>.

Mills, C. (2008). Making a difference: Moving beyond the superficial treatment of diversity. *Asia-Pacific Journal of Teacher Education, 36*(4), 261–75.

— (2009). Making sense of pre-service teachers' dispositions towards social justice: Can teacher education make a difference? *Critical Studies in Education, 50*(3), 277–88.

— (2012). When 'picking the right people' is not enough: A Bourdieuian analysis of social justice and dispositional change in pre-service teachers. *International Journal of Educational Research, 53,* 269–77.

Mills, C., & Ballantyne, J. (2010, April). Pre-service teachers' dispositions towards diversity: Arguing for a developmental hierarchy of change. *Teaching and Teacher Education, 26*(3), 447–54.

Milner, H. (2010). What does teacher education have to do with teaching? *Journal of Teacher Education, 61*(1), 118–31.

Mirza, H. (1992). *Young, female and Black.* London: Routledge.

— (2009). *Race, gender and educational desire: Why Black women succeed and fail.* London: Routledge.

Modood, T. (1998). 'Racial equality: Colour, culture and justice. In J. Franklin (Ed.), *Social policy and social justice* (pp. 167–81). Cambridge: Polity Press.

— (2006). Ethnicity and higher education in Britain. *Teaching in Higher Education, 11*(2), 247–50.

— (2007). *Multiculturalism: A civic idea.* Bristol: Polity Press.

Modood, T., & Shiner, M. (2002). Help or hindrance? Higher education and the route to ethnic equality. *British Journal of Sociology of Education*, 23(2), 209–32.

Moodie, G. (2012a, 30 January). University types. Retrieved from http://rmit.academia.edu/GavinMoodie/Papers/265078/Types_of_Australian_universities

— (2012b). Variations in the rate at which students cross the boundaries between Australian vocational and higher education. *Australian Educational Researcher, 39*(2), 143–58.

Moran, A. (2011). Multiculturalism as nation-building in Australia: Inclusive national identity and the embrace of diversity. *Ethnic and Racial Studies, 34*(12), 2153–72.

Moreton-Robinson, A. (Ed.) (2004). *Whitening race: Essays in social and cultural criticism.* Canberra, ACT, Australia: Aboriginal Studies Press.

Moses, A. D. (2010). Time, indigeneity, and peoplehood: The postcolony in Australia. *Postcolonial Studies, 13*(1), 9–32.

Moule, J. (2005, Fall). Implementing a social justice perspective in education. *Teacher Education Quarterly,* 23–42.

Myers, K. (2009). Immigrants and ethnic minorities in the history of education. *Paedagogica Historica: International Journal of the History of Education, 45*(6), 801–16.

Myers, S. M. (2005). *Students at risk and higher education: Does civic and school involvement lead to improved college plans, awareness and preparation?* Annual meeting of the Pacific Sociological Association, Portland, OR (April).

Nama, A. (2011). *Super Black: American pop culture and Black superheroes.* Austin, TX: University of Texas Press.

Naples, N. A. (2008). *Crossing borders: Feminism, intersectionality and globalisation (Hawke Research Institute working paper series no. 36).* Magill, SA, Australia: Hawke Research Institute for Sustainable Societies, University of South Australia.

The National Committee of Inquiry into Higher Education. (1997). *The Dearing Report.* HMSO: London.

Nayak, A. (2003). *Race, place and globalisation: Youth cultures in a changing world.* Oxford: Berg.

Neal, S. (2002). Rural landscapes, representations and racism: Examining multicultural citizenship and policy-making in the English countryside. *Ethnic and Racial Studies, 25*(3), 442–61.

Nelson, A. (2009, April). Learning from the past, looking to the future: Exploring our place with Indigenous Australians. *Australian Occupational Therapy Journal, 56*(2), 97–102.

Neumann, R., & Guthrie, J. (2002, October). The corporatization of research in Australian higher education. *Critical Perspectives on Accounting, 13*(5–6), 721–41.

Nickolai, D. H., Hoffman, S. G., & Trautner, M. N. (2012, March). Can a knowledge sanctuary also be an economic engine? The marketization of higher education as institutional boundary work. *Sociology Compass, 6*(3), 205–18.

Nieto, S. (2001). What keeps teachers going in spite of everything? And other thoughts on the future of public education. *Journal of Equity and Excellence in Education, 34*(1), 6–15.

— (2006). *Teaching as political work: Learning from courageous and caring teachers.* Child Development Occasional Paper Series. New York: Routledge.

— (2010). *Literacy and culture at the school: Language, culture, and teaching: Critical perspectives.* London and New York: Routledge.

Nussbaum, M. C. (2003). Capabilities as fundamental entitlements: Sen and social justice. *Feminist Economics, 9*(2–3), 33–59.

Nuttall, J., & Ortlipp, M. (2012). Practicum assessment of culturally and linguistically diverse early childhood pre-service teachers. *European Early Childhood Education Research Journal, 20*(1), 47–60.

Olmedo, I., & Harbon, L. (2010). Broadening our sights: Internationalizing teacher education for a global arena. *Teaching Education, 21*(1), 75–88.

O'Neill, B. (2011, Winter). Anti-discrimination law and the attack on freedom of conscience. *Policy, 27*(2), 3–8.

Orfield, G. (2001). *Schools more separate: Consequences of a decade of resegregation.* Cambridge, MA: The Civil Rights Project at Harvard University.

Papadopoulos, I., & Lees, S. (2002). Developing culturally competent researchers. *Journal of Advanced Nursing, 37*(3), 258–64.

Pardy, M., & Lee, J. C. H. (2011). Using buzzwords of belonging: Everyday multiculturalism and social capital in Australia. *Journal of Australian Studies, 35*(3), 297–316.

Parekh, B. (2006). *Rethinking multiculturalism.* London: Palgrave.

— (2008). *A new politics of identity: Political principles for an interdependent world.* Basingstoke, UK: Palgrave Macmillan.

Parkinson, P. (2007). Religious vilification, anti-discrimination laws and religious minorities in Australia: The freedom to be different. *Australian Law Journal, 81*(12), 954–66.

Pathak, S. (2000). *Race research for the future ethnicity in education training and the labour market* (Research Topic Paper RTP01) Nottingham: DfES.

Phelan, M. (1997). Power and place. *Teaching and Teacher Education, 17*(5), 583–97.

Phoenix, A. (1987). Theories of gender and Black families. In Gaby Weiner & Madeleine Arnot (Eds.), *Gender under scrutiny: New inquiries in education* (pp. 50–61). London: Hutchinson.

— (2009). De-colonising practices: Negotiating narratives from racialized and gendered experiences of education. *Race Ethnicity and Education, 12*(1), 101–14.

Pini, B., Price, R., & McDonald, P. (2010). Teachers and the emotional dimensions of class in resource-affected rural Australia. *British Journal of Sociology of Education, 31*(1), 17–30.

Poed, S., & Keen, D. A. (2009). Reasonable adjustment? The intersection between Australian disability discrimination legislation and parental perceptions of curriculum adjustments in Queensland schools. In B. Garrick, S. Poed, & J. Skinner (Eds.), *Educational planet shapers: Researching, hypothesising, dreaming the future* (pp. 81–96). Brisbane, Qld, Australia: Post Pressed.

Powney, J., Wilson, V., Hall, S., Davidson, J., Kirk, J., & Edward, S. with Mirza, H. (2003). *Teachers' careers: The impact of age, disability, ethnicity, gender and sexual orientation.* Research Report RR488. Nottingham: Department for Education and Skills.

Preston, J. (2007). *Whiteness and class in education.* Dordrecht: Springer.

Pugliese, J., & Stryker, S. (2009). The somatechnics of race and whiteness. *Social Semiotics, 19*(1), 1–8.

Putman, T., & Gill, J. (2011). The Bradley challenge: A sea change for Australian universities? *Issues in Educational Research, 21*(2), 176–91.

Race into Higher Education (2010). Communities and Local Government: London.

Race Relations Amendment Act (2000). HMSO: London.

Rahier, J., Hintzen, P., & Smith, F. (Eds.), *Global circuits of Blackness: Interrogating the African diaspora*. Urbana-Champaign, IL: University of Illinois Press.

Ramsey, P. G., & Williams, L. R. (2003). *Multicultural education: A source book*. (2nd edition). New York: Routledge.

Ramzan, B., Pini, B., & Bryant, L. (2009, October). Experiencing and writing Indigeneity, rurality and gender: Australian reflections. *Journal of Rural Studies, 25*(4), 435–43.

Raphael, J., & Allard, A. C. (2012/in press). Positioning people with intellectual disabilities as the experts: Enhancing pre-service teachers' competencies in teaching for diversity. *International Journal of Inclusive Education*.

Rawls, J. (2001). *Justice as fairness*. Harvard: Harvard University Press.

Reay, D. (1995). They employ cleaners to do that: Habitus in the primary classroom. *British Journal of Sociology of Education, 16*(3), 353–71.

Reay, D., David, M., & Ball, S. (2005). *Degrees of choice: Social class, race and gender in higher education*. Stoke-on-Trent: Trentham.

Reay, D., Ball, S. J., David, M., & Davies, J. (2001). Choices of degree or degrees of choice? Social class, race and the higher education choice process. *Sociology, 35*(4), 855–74.

Reay, D., Hollingworth, S., Williams, K., Crozier, G., Jamieson, F., James, D., & Beedell, P. (2007, December). 'A darker shade of pale?' Whiteness, the middle classes and multi-ethnic inner city schooling. *Sociology, 41*(6), 1041–60.

Reid, C., & Sriprakash, A. (2012). The possibility of cosmopolitan learning: Reflecting on future directions for diversity teacher education in Australia. *Asia-Pacific Journal of Teacher Education, 40*(1), 15–29.

Reid, C., & Young, H. (2012/forthcoming). The new compulsory schooling age policy in NSW. Australia: Ethnicity, ability and gender considerations. *Journal of Education Policy*.

Reinharz, S. (1986). *Feminist methods in social research*. New York: Oxford University Press.

Report of the Committee on Higher Education. (1963). *The Robbins Report*. HMSO: London.

Reynolds, H. (2006). *The other side of the frontier: Aboriginal resistance to the European invasion of Australia*. Sydney, NSW, Australia: University of New South Wales Press.

Reynolds, R., & Brown, J. (2010). Social justice and school linkages in teacher education programmes. *European Journal of Teacher Education, 33*(4), 405–19.

Rhamie, J. (2007). *Eagles who soar*. Stoke-on-Trent: Trentham.

Rhamie, J., Bhopal, K., & Bhatti, G. (2012). Stick to your own kind: Pupils' experiences of identity and diversity in secondary schools. *British Journal of Educational Studies, 60*(2), 171–91.

Richardson, L. (2000, June). Evaluating ethnography. *Qualitative Inquiry, 6*(2), 253–55.

Richardson, R., & Wood, A. (1999). *Inclusive schools, inclusive society: Race and identity on the agenda.* Stoke-on-Trent: Trentham.

Riessman, C. K. (1987). When gender is not enough. *Gender & Society, 1*(2), 172–207.

Robertson, S. (2000). Re-imagining and rescripting the future of education: Global knowledge economy discourses and the challenge to education systems. *Comparative Education, 41*(2), 151–70.

— (2011). Cash cows, backdoor migrants, or activist citizens? International students, citizenship, and rights in Australia. *Ethnic and Racial Studies, 34*(12), 2192–211.

Robinson, K. H., & Ferfolja, T. (2008, May). Playing it up, playing it down, playing it safe: Queering teacher education. *Teaching and Teacher Education, 24*(4), 846–58.

Rodrigues, M. (2003). *Citizenship and the political institutions of cultural diversity in Australia.* Unpublished Doctor of Philosophy dissertation, School of Social and International Studies, Faculty of Arts, Deakin University, Geelong, Vic, Australia.

Roediger, D. (1992). *The wages of Whiteness.* New York: Verso.

— (1994). *Towards the abolition of Whiteness.* New York: Verso.

Ross, M., Grace, D., & Shao, W. (2012/in press). Come on higher ed . . . get with the programme! A study of market orientation in international student recruitment. *Educational Review.*

Rowlands, J. (2012/in press). Academic boards: Less intellectual and more academic capital in higher education governance? *Studies in Higher Education.*

Russell, S. (2006). *Evaluation of national science foundation support for undergraduate research opportunities.* Higher Education Funding Council for England.

Ryan, M., & Healy, A. (2009, April). It's not all about school: Ways of disrupting pre-service teachers' perceptions of pedagogy and communication. *Teaching and Teacher Education, 25*(3), 424–9.

Ryan, M., Carrington, S., Selva, G., & Healy, A. (2009). Taking a 'reality' check: Expanding pre-service teachers' views on pedagogy and diversity. *Asia-Pacific Journal of Teacher Education, 37*(2), 155–73.

Sabatini Sloan, A. (2010, Fall). A forecast for Blackness: The work of Victor LaValle. *Callaloo, 33*(4), 879–981.

Saethre, E. (2009). Medical interactions, complaints, and the construction of Aboriginality in remote Australia. *Social Identities: Journal for the Study of Race, Nation and Culture, 15*(6), 773–86.

Santoro, N. (2009). 'She's one of us': Ethnic minority and Indigenous teachers in culturally diverse Australian classrooms. In F. Mansouri (Ed.), *Youth identity and migration: Culture, values and social connectedness* (pp. 87–104). Altona, Vic: Common Ground.

Santoro, N., & Allard, A. (2006). Creating spaces for learning: Research as pedagogy. *Australian Educational Researcher, 33*(1), 41–54.

Santoro, N., & Snead, S. L. (2012/in press). 'I'm not a real academic': A career from industry to academe. *Journal of Further and Higher Education.*

Santoro, N., Reid, J.-A., Crawford, L., & Simpson, L. (2012). Teaching Indigenous teachers: Valuing diverse perspectives. In T. N. Basit & S. Tomlinson (Eds.), *Social inclusion and higher education* (pp. 255–72). Bristol, UK: Policy Press.

Santoro, N., Reid, J.-A., Mayer, D., & Singh, M. (2012). Producing 'quality' teachers: The role of teacher professional standards. *Asia-Pacific Journal of Teacher Education, 40*(1), 1–3.

Savage, G. C. (2011, January). When worlds collide: Excellent and equitable learning communities? Australia's 'social capitalist' paradox. *Journal of Education Policy, 26*(1), 33–59.

Sellar, S., & Gale, T. (2011). Mobility, aspiration, voice: A new structure of feeling for student equity in higher education. *Critical Studies in Education, 52*(2), 115–34.

Serafini, F. (2001). *The reading workshop: Creating space for readers.* Portsmouth, NH: Heinemann.

Shah, M., & Widin, J. (2010, September). Indigenous students' voices: Monitoring student satisfaction and retention in a large Australian university. *Journal of Institutional Research, 15*(1), 28–41.

Shih, M., & Sanchez, D. T. (2009, March). When race becomes even more complex: Toward understanding the landscape of multiracial identity and experiences. *Journal of Social Issues, 65*(1), 1–11.

Shore, S. (2010, Spring). Whiteness at work in vocational training in Australia. *New Directions for Adult and Continuing Education, 2010*(125), 41–51.

Sieber, J., & Stanley, B. (1988). 'Ethical and professional dimensions of socially sensitive research. *American Psychologist, 42*, 49–55.

Simmel, G. (1950). The stranger from Kurt Wolff (Trans.). *The sociology of George Simmel.* New York: Free Press.

Singh, M. (2009). Using Chinese knowledge in internationalising research education: Jacques Rancière, an ignorant supervisor and doctoral students from China. *Globalisation, Societies and Education, 7*(2), 185–201.

Skelton, C., Francis, B., & Valkanova, Y. (2007). *Breaking down the stereotypes: Gender and achievement in schools.* Manchester: Equal Opportunities Commission.

Skills in the global economy. (2004). London: HMSO.

Sleeter, C. E. (2001). *Culture, difference and power.* New York: Teachers College Press.

— (2005). *Un-Standardizing curriculum: Multicultural teaching in standards-based classrooms.* New York: Teachers College Press.

— (Ed.) (2007). *Facing accountability in education: Democracy and equity at risk.* New York: Teachers College Press.

Sleeter, C. E., & Grant, C. A. (2009). *Making choices for multicultural education: Five approaches to race, class and gender* (6th edition). Chichester: Wiley Press.

Smith, B., & Allen, D. (2012). Whose fault is it? Asking the right questions when trying to address discrimination. *Alternative Law Journal, 37*(1), 31–6.

Smolicz, J., & Secombe, M. (2009). Globalisation, identity, and cultural dynamics in a multi-ethnic state: Multiculturalism in Australia. In J. Zajda, H. Daun, & L. J. Saha

(Eds.), *Nation-building, identity and citizenship education: Cross-cultural perspectives (Globalisation, comparative education and policy research vol. 3)* (pp. 83–98). Dordrecht, The Netherlands: Springer.

Song, M. (2003). *Choosing ethnic identity*. London: Sage.

Song, M., & Parker, D. (1985). Commonality, difference and the dynamics of disclosure in in-depth interviewing. *Sociology, 29*(2), 241–56.

Soto, I., & Showers Johnson, V. (Eds.) (2012). *Western fictions, Black realities: Meanings of Blackness and modernities*. East Lansing, MI: Michigan State University Press.

Souto-Manning, M. (2011). Playing with power and privilege: Theatre games in teacher education. *Teaching and Teacher Education, 27*(6), 997–1007.

Spivak, G. (1999). *A critique of postcolonial realism*. Harvard: Harvard University Press.

Steedman, H. (2010). To avoid creating a 'lost generation', with perhaps a fifth of all 18 year olds unemployed and outside training, a new push on apprenticeships would help. Retrieved from http://eprints.lse.ac.uk/39711/1/blogs.lse.ac.uk-To_avoid_creating_a_lost_generation_with_perhaps_a_fifth_of_all_18_year_olds_unemployed_and_outside_t.pdf

Stevenson, J., & Lang, M. (2010). *Social class and higher education*. London: Higher Education Academy.

Stoer, S., & Cortesao, L. (2000). Multiculturalism and educational policy in a global content (European perspectives). In N. Burbules & C. A. Torres (Eds.), *Globalization and education: Critical perspectives*. New York: Routledge.

Stratton, J. (2004). Borderline anxieties: What whitening the Irish has to do with keeping out asylum seekers. In A. Moreton-Robinson (Ed.), *Whitening race: Essays in social and cultural criticism* (pp. 222–38). Canberra, ACT, Australia: Aboriginal Studies Press.

Sturman, A. (1997). *Social justice in education*. Melbourne: ACER.

Sutton Trust. (2004). The missing 3000 – state schools under-represented at leading universities. www.suttontrust.com/research/the-missing-3000/

Syed, J., & Kramar, R. (2009). What is the Australian model for managing cultural diversity? *Personnel Review, 39*(1), 96–115.

Tascón, S. M. (2008). Narratives of race and nation: Everyday Whiteness in Australia. *Social Identities: Journal for the Study of Race, Nation and Culture, 14*(2), 253–74.

Tate, W. (1997). Critical race theory and education: History, theory and implications. *Review of Research in Education, 22*, 191–243.

Theobald, S. (2011). Should I pitch my tent in the middle ground? On 'middling tendency', Beck and inequality in youth sociology. *Journal of Youth Studies, 14*(4), 381–93.

Thomas, S., & Hay, S. (2012). Governing schooling, people and practices: Australian policies on transitions. In S. Billett, G. Johnson, S. Thomas, C. Sim, S. Hay, & J. Ryan (Eds.), *Experiences of school transitions: Policies, practice and participants* (pp. 141–61). Dordrecht, The Netherlands: Springer.

Threadgold, S., & Nilan, P. (2009, January). Reflexivity of contemporary youth, risk and cultural capital. *Current Sociology, 57*(1), 47–68.

Tolley, J., & Rundle, J. (2006). *A review of Black and minority ethnic participation in higher education*. London: Aimhigher.

Tomlinson, S. (2005). *Education in a post welfare society*. Milton Keynes: Open University Press.

Toombs, M., & Gorman, D. (2011). Mental health and Indigenous university students. *Aboriginal and Islander Health Worker Journal, 35*(4), 22–4.

Tracy, S. J., & Trethewey, A. (2005). Fracturing the real-self↔fake-self dichotomy: Moving toward 'crystallized' organizational discourses and identities. *Communication Theory, 15*, 168–95.

Training and Development Agency. (2003). Annual Statistics.

—. (2007). Annual Statistics.

—. (2009). Annual Statistics.

Turner, R. (2000). Gypsies and politics in Britain. *Political Quarterly, 71*(1), 77–118.

Tyler, S. (2011). Transforming inequality in the classroom: Not as easy as it sounds. *Journal of Student Engagement Education Matters, 1*(1), 21–8.

Universities Australia. (2012, February). University profiles. Retrieved from www. universitiesaustralia.edu.au/page/australia-s-universities/university-profiles/

University of Leicester Research Paper (2010). *Raising the fee cap*.

Vakalahi, H. F. O., & Ihara, E. S. (2011). Research with Indigenous cultures: A case study analysis of Tongan grandparents. *Families in Society: The Journal of Contemporary Social Services, 92*(2), 230–5.

van Wormer, K. (2009). Restorative justice as social justice for victims of gendered violence: A standpoint feminist perspective. *Social Work, 54*(2), 107–16.

Vass, G. (2012/in press). The racialised educational landscape in Australia: Listening to the whispering elephant. *Race ethnicity and education*.

Villegas, A. M., & Davis, D. E. (2008). Preparing teachers of color to confront racial/ ethnic disparities in educational outcomes. In M. Cochran-Smith, S. Feiman-Nemser, D. J. McIntyre, & K. Demers (Eds.), *Handbook on research in teacher education* (pp. 583–605). New York: Routledge.

Wang, J. (2012, April). Culturally inclusive practice: A case study of an international student support initiative at an Australian university. *Asian Social Science, 8*(4), 68–76.

Ware, V., & Black, L. (2002). *Out of Whiteness*. Chicago: University of Chicago Press.

Watts, M. (2012). *Accessing elite universities: Capability, capital and widening participation*. Dordrecht, The Netherlands: Springer.

Whitford, T. A. (2011). A civil conflict: National action, immigration and multiculturalism in Australia. *Rural Society, 20*(2).

Whitington, V., Ebbeck, M., Diamond, A., & Yim, H. Y. B. (2009, March). A pathway to enhancing professionalism: Building a bridge between TAFE and university early childhood qualifications. *Australasian Journal of Early Childhood, 34*(1), 27–35.

Wilkins, C. (2001). Student teachers and attitudes towards 'race': The role of citizenship education in addressing racism through the curriculum. *Westminster Studies in Education, 24*(1), 7–21.

Williams, G., & Filippakou, O. (2010). Higher education and UK elite formation in the twentieth century. *Higher Education, 59*(1), 1–20.

Williams, M. (2009, 1 December). The White woman's burden: Whiteness and the neo-colonialist historical imagination in *The Proposition* (John Hillcoat, 2005). *Studies in Australasian Cinema, 3*(3), 265–78.

Willmott, H. (1995). Managing the academics: Commodification and control in the development of university education in the UK. *Human Relations, 48*(9), 993–1028.

Windle, J. (2008). The management and legitimisation of educational inequalities in Australia: Some implications for school experience. *International Studies in Sociology of Education, 18*(3–4), 157–71.

Wohling, M. (2009). The problem of scale in Indigenous knowledge: A perspective from Northern Australia. *Ecology and Society, 14*(1). Retrieved from www.ecologyandsociety.org/vol14/iss1/art1/

Wood, D., & Willems, J. (2012). Responding to the widening participation agenda through improved access to and within 3D virtual learning environments. *Australasian Journal of Educational Technology, 28*(3), 459–79.

Woodcock, S., Hemmings, B., & Kay, R. (2012, June). Does study of an inclusive education subject influence pre-service teachers' concerns and self-efficacy about inclusion? *Australian Journal of Teacher Education, 37*(6), article 1.

Wray, M., & Newitz, A. (1997). *White trash: Race and class in America.* New York: Routledge.

Wright, R. R., & Sandin, J. A. (2009, February). Cult TV, hip hop, shape-shifters, and vampire slayers. *Adult Education Quarterly, 59*(2), 118–41.

Xiao, H., & Petraki, E. (2007). An investigation of Chinese students' difficulties in intercultural communication and its role in ELT. *Journal of Intercultural Communication*, 13, article 5. Retrieved from www.immi.se/jicc/index.php/jicc/issue/view/11

Yep, K. S. (2012). Peddling sport: Liberal multiculturalism and the racial triangulation of Blackness, Chineseness and Native American-ness in professional basketball. *Ethnic and Racial Studies, 35*(6), 971–87.

Yoon, B., Simpson, A., & Haag, C. (2010, October). Assimilation ideology: Critically examining underlying messages in multicultural literature. *Journal of Adolescent & Adult Literacy, 54*(2), 109–18.

Youdell, D. (2006). Diversity, inequality and a post-structural politics for education. *Discourse: Studies in the cultural politics of education, 27*(1), 33–42.

Young, D. (2011, June). Mutable things: Colours as material practice in the northwest of South Australia. *Journal of the Royal Anthropological Institute, 17*(2), 356–76.

Young, I. (1990). *Justice and the politics of difference.* Princeton: Princeton University Press.

Young, S., & Zubrzycki, J. (2011, April). Educating Australian social workers in the post-Apology era: The potential offered by a 'Whiteness' lens. *Journal of Social work, 11*(2), 159–73.

Zajda, J., Biraimah, B., & Gaudelli, W (Eds.) (2008). *Education and social inequality in the global culture* (pp. xvii–xxvii). Dordrecht: Springer.

Zeichner, K. (2001). Educational action research. In P. Reason & H. Bradbury (Eds.), *Action research – participative inquiry and practice*. London: Sage.

— (2009). *Teacher education and the struggle for social justice*. New York: Routledge.

Zevallos, Z. (2008). 'You have to be Anglo and not look like me': Identity and belonging among young women of Turkish and Latin American backgrounds in Melbourne, Australia. *Australian Geographer, 39*(1), 21–43.

Zhou, Y., Windsor, C., Theobald, K., & Coyer, F. (2011, November). The concept of difference and the experience of China-educated nurses working in Australia: A symbolic interactionist exploration. *International Journal of Nursing Studies, 48*(11), 1420–8.

Zuber-Skerritt, O., & Kearney, J. (2012). Participatory action learning and action research for sustainable migrant community development. In O. Zuber-Skerritt (Ed.), *Action research for sustainable development in a turbulent world* (pp. 167–88). Bingley, UK: Emerald Group Publishing.

Zumwalt, K., & Craig, E. (2005). Teachers' characteristics: Research on the demographic profile. In M. Cochran-Smith & K. M. Zeichner (Eds.), *Studying teacher education* (pp. 111–56). Washington, DC: American Educational Research Association.

Index

Lightning Source UK Ltd.
Milton Keynes UK
UKHW02f0240161018
330622UK00005B/117/P